W9-CEH-267

The Electric Slow Cooker Cookbook

The Electric Slow Cooker Cookbook

Barbara Bean

Henry Regnery Company • Chicago

Library of Congress Cataloging in Publication Data

Bean, Barbara.
The electric slow cooker cookbook

1. Cookery. 2. Casserole receipts. I. Title.
TX652.B337 1975 641.5'86 75-13212
ISBN 0-8092-8232-1
ISBN 0-8092-8146-5 pbk.

The author wishes to thank the many people who assisted in the preparation of this book, especially Mary Esther Croker, Sherill Shreefer, Maureen Pischke, Marian Faux, Stephen B. Croker, Nancy Bush, and Emily Douglass.

Published by Henry Regnery Company
180 North Michigan Avenue, Chicago, Illinois 60601
Manufactured in the United States of America
Library of Congress Catalog Card Number: 75-13212
International Standard Book Number: 0-8092-8232-1 (cloth)
0-8092-8146-5 (paper)

Published simultaneously in Canada by
Fitzhenry & Whiteside Limited
150 Lesmill Road
Don Mills, Ontario M3B 2T5
Canada

Contents

Introduction

Until the invention of the slow cooker, the only way you could come home to a fully cooked, ready-to-serve meal was to hire a cook. Unfortunately, most of us cannot afford that luxury. For those who work or are involved in a wide variety of activities outside the home, cooking quick, interesting, and nutritious meals has become a problem.

The answer for many has been to buy convenience foods. But most people have discovered that "convenient" is not the same as "quick." Even frozen dinners take at least half an hour to prepare. Also, most convenience foods are expensive and highly caloric, and the variety is limited.

The electric slow cooker promises true convenience, geared to today's hectic lifestyles. It is a descendent of the large iron pot that once hung over an open household fire simmering foods gently all day long and is directly adapted from the bean pot, which squatted all day and night on the back burner of grandmother's stove. A slow cooker also cooks all day, but with one important difference: it cooks unattended while you are away from home. When you walk in the door at the end of the day, the meal is ready to serve.

Since a slow cooker cooks foods at low temperatures in a covered container to retain moisture, cooking time can vary by several hours with no difference in taste or appearance. What's more, most slow-cooker meals can be prepared easily; many involve nothing more than putting all the ingredients into the pot at one time, covering it, and setting the proper temperature.

There are two other reasons why this newest home appliance has grown so rapidly in popularity: economy and nutrition. The slow cooker is economical because it uses very little electricity (usually less than a nickel a day), tenderizes less expensive cuts of meat and poultry, and minimizes meat shrinkage.

Nutritionists praise the slow cooker because it retains vital nutrients. The low temperature at which the food is cooked destroys fewer heat-sensitive nutrients, and nutrients that pass into the cooking liquid usually are saved because most slow cooker recipes use the pot liquor as a sauce or gravy.

This cookbook includes kitchen-tested recipes of all types, adapted for slow cooker use. Many recipes are modernized versions of dishes from around the world that were originally cooked all day in the large iron kettles of old. They restore the true, simmered-for-hours flavor of these old favorites without the hard work.

The French have the ideal expression for the slow cooking that develops such marvelous flavors; their idiomatic expression for a "low simmer" translates literally as "making the pot smile." I hope that this collection of recipes will produce the same result in your kitchen.

1

A Quick Lesson in Slow Cooking

Understanding the peculiarities of and special techniques used in slow cooking will help you get more flavorful results and better value for your food dollar.

For example, some types of food are more suitable for slow cooking than others. You would be wasting your money to cook a prime rib in the slow cooker; it tastes best when dry roasted at a high temperature so the outside has a crisp crust and the inside is rare and juicy. On the other hand, the texture and flavor of the less expensive chuck roast is enhanced by many hours of moist cooking that slowly break down tough muscle fibers. Certain foods will not hold up in all-day cooking and may have to be added at the end of the cooking period. Amounts of seasonings and liquids also differ from those used in other cooking methods.

You can use the recipes in this book just as they are printed since they are specifically designed for slow cooker use. However, to adapt your favorite recipes to the slow cooker you will have to make certain changes. The cooking hints in this chapter will help you prepare the recipes in this book and adapt your own recipes as well.

Understanding How a Slow Cooker Works

All slow cookers are electrically operated, cook foods at low temperatures (usually 200° to 300°) for many hours, and have a cover to seal in moisture. Apart from these common features, however, they differ in style, size, shape, and construction. If you already own a slow cooker, you should become familiar with its features. If you are shopping for a slow cooker, look for the following characteristics:

Capacity and Shape. The average-sized slow cooker is approximately 3½ quarts, large enough to cook meals for from 4 to 6 people. Larger models, 4½ quarts to 8 quarts, will serve 6 to 12 people. Small 2-quart cookers are adequate for a couple's meals but seldom hold enough for company dinners. It might make more sense for a couple who entertains frequently to buy the 3½-quart model and freeze leftovers. Choosing the slow cooker's shape—round and "pot shaped," oval or casserole style—is purely a matter of personal preference.

Temperature ranges and heat controls. Slow cookers have several different types of heat controls. Some have snap-in detents with "Low-Medium-High" or "Off-Low-High" settings. Others have a dial control so you can select any temperature within a certain range. Temperatures are usually indicated on the control or in the use-and-care book accompanying the slow cooker. Some slow cookers operate only at slow-cooking temperature ranges—190° to 300°. Others also offer a very low temperature range for warming foods and/or an extra-hot setting up to 500° for browning and frying.

The "warm" setting should never be used for cooking. Perishable foods must be cooked at a temperature of at least 165° maintained for two hours or more to kill harmful bacteria. If you use a model with low-temperature settings, make sure you always cook at temperature ranges of 170° or above.

Models with the high-temperature ranges use more electricity, but they do combine two types of cooking in one appliance. If you have this type cooker, however, be sure to check that it is at a low setting before you leave the slow cooker unattended; foods will burn when left unattended at the higher temperature settings.

Whatever the type of heat control on the model you choose, find out the temperatures it reaches at each setting. If temperatures are not printed on the dial, look in the use-and-care book accompanying the appliance. This is the only way to compare times with recipes in this book. *The* Low *setting used in the recipes in this book is 200°.* The High *setting is 300°.* You will have to adjust cooking times slightly if your slow cooker cooks at different temperatures.

Materials. Slow cookers are often made from a combination of materials. Exterior surfaces are usually steel, aluminum, baked enamel, or rugged, heat-resistant plastic. Interior containers (which may or may not be removable) are made of stoneware, heat-resistant plastic, aluminum, glass, or porcelain enamel, with or without a non-stick finish.

Stoneware retains flavors and juices better than other materials, but it may be slightly more difficult to clean and may crack with sudden changes in temperature or a sharp blow. Both stoneware and glass cook more evenly than metal.

Construction. The important difference in construction among various models is the position of the heating element. In some the heating element is wrapped around the sides, between exterior and interior containers. In others it is coiled in the bottom beneath the interior container. The side-wrapped element tends to cook more evenly, preventing foods from burning. The base element usually offers a wider range of temperatures.

Other construction characteristics to note are stability, exterior temperature, and portability. Cookers should not tip easily or slide when placed on a slightly tilted counter top. Cookers with handles near the top are easiest to carry. Some users, particularly those with young children, may also want to check to see if the temperature of the exterior container becomes too hot to touch after several hours of cooking. Another safety feature is a device that lets you turn off the cooker by some other method than pulling out the cord. A slow cooker definitely should carry the UL seal, signifying that the appliance meets the safety standards of Underwriters' Laboratories.

Convenience Features. Look for features that make cleaning easy, such as a removable heat control, removable inner container, or a fully immersible cooker. Another handy feature is a glass or plastic transparent cover that lets you see the food without removing the lid. Some slow cookers now offer cooking accessories for certain types of food—vegetable steamers, cake bakers, and other specialty items that make slow cooking more convenient.

Learning to Use the Slow Cooker

One key to the slow cooker's convenience is flexibility of cooking time. Most models let you cook a dish at one of several temperatures. The most common settings are Low and High, with foods taking twice as long to cook on Low as on High. You may cook a pot roast for 8-10 hours on Low, or 4-5 hours on High, depending on which best suits your schedule. (A model with a dial control lets you cook at any temperature within the given range, allowing even greater flexibility.)

This two hour or more spread may seem vague, but timing is not crucial in slow cooking because temperatures are low and foods do not burn even if cooked a few hours longer than the suggested maximum. If you leave home at 9 a.m. and return about 6 p.m., you set the slow cooker on Low to cook a recipe 8-10 hours. Even if you arrive home an hour earlier or later than you had planned, your dinner will be ready to serve upon your arrival.

Even greater flexibility is possible by combining High and Low settings. Say a recipe calls for cooking on Low 8-10 hours (High: 4-5 hours), but you want to eat in 6 hours. Cook on High for 3 hours (equal to 6 hours on Low), then turn to Low for the additional 2-4 hours of cooking required. (Cooking time may vary somewhat because of voltage variations or variations in altitude and humidity.)

At the beginning of each chapter, general directions explain which types of foods adapt best to slow cooking. Some foods are not suitable for all-day cooking: rice (except long grain), noodles, macaroni, seafood, Chinese vegetables, and milk. These foods should not be cooked longer than six hours and usually should be added to the slow cooker two hours before serving. If you will not be home to add these foods later, cook on High for a shorter time, or use a substitute food. You can substitute evaporated milk or a condensed cream soup for homogenized milk for all-day cooking. Or, make a white sauce with milk and flour before adding the milk to the other ingredients. You can cook rice and macaroni before you add them to other ingredients; if you add them raw, add an extra cup of liquid in addition to what the recipe already calls for. Long grain and wild rice, which can be cooked all-day, may be substituted for white rice.

Because the cover seals in moisture and because foods are cooked at low temperatures, liquids do not boil away in the slow cooker. Therefore, you add less liquid at the beginning than you would in a normal recipe. If, after cooking a recipe for the required length of time, you find that there is too much liquid remaining, remove the cover and turn the slow cooker to High for 45 minutes to 1 hour. Sauces and gravies can be made from a thin pot liquor by adding a thickening agent such as flour and water, flour and butter, or cornstarch.

Correct seasoning of foods will take some practice in slow cooking. In many slow cooker recipes, several foods are cooked together and the blended flavors result in a natural seasoning. These recipes may not require as much salt, pepper, or fresh herbs and spices but will require slightly more ground spices. If you are home you may want to wait until the last hour of cooking to add ground spices so their flavors will be at a peak.

Other tips you might find useful in slow cooking . . .

• If you are cooking on High, stir the ingredients occasionally. There should be no need to stir on Low, although you might have to if you are using a slow cooker that has the heating element in the bottom.

• Slow cookers, unlike other types of cooking vessels, cook meat more quickly than vegetables. For this reason, it is best to quarter vegetables or cut them in smaller pieces and place the vegetables in the bottom or around the sides where they will cook faster.

• Some foods lose color after long hours of slow cooking. Foods like fresh mushrooms, or frozen peas or corn can be added during the last hour, if convenient, to preserve their full color.

• If you want a crisp topping on a dish, you should add it about a half hour before serving and cook the dish for the remaining time without the cover. Many dishes are improved with a topping of bread crumbs or bacon bits. Biscuit or mashed-potato toppings have to be cooked in the oven, which means you have to transfer the dish from the slow cooker to a baking dish to finish it. It is easier to substitute another topping.

• Single persons and couples will have leftovers from many of the recipes in this book. Leftovers can be frozen using directions given in most general cookbooks (see special freezing hints for soups in the introduction to Chapter 2). If you use leftovers within a few days, you may reheat them in the slow cooker. Cook them for half the time required for the original recipe.

• If you are cooking a recipe in this book in a 2-quart slow cooker, you should halve the recipe. Depending on how many people you plan to serve, you can cook a recipe as is for a 4½-quart slow cooker, or make 1½ to 2 times as much. For 8-quart models, double the recipes. Regardless of the size of the slow cooker, recipes should take approximately the same amount of time to cook. Check the book that comes with the appliance for suggestions on cooking times.

Since many of the foods that can be prepared in the slow cooker can be cooked in other ways, too, you should decide which is the most convenient method. It may seem foolish to you to bake a loaf of bread in a slow cooker when you can easily bake it in the oven for 45 minutes the night before. There may be times, however, when it is easier for you to prepare a bread in the slow cooker so you can leave home and have it ready when you return. It is nice to have the choice; you will especially appreciate being able to cook those only-on-Sunday roasts on any workday.

Cleaning and Caring For Your Slow Cooker

Read the book that comes with your slow cooker for care cleaning instructions. Most slow cookers are easily cleaned; some can even be fully immersed in the sink. If foods stick to the sides, just add warm water and soak for several hours before cleaning. Be sure to follow any special care instructions. Some slow cookers will crack if subjected to sudden changes in temperature or a sharp blow. Some have special finishes that could be damaged by harsh cleansers. Your cooker will last much longer if you care for it properly.

To Use the Recipes in This Book

Unless otherwise noted, the recipes in this book are designed for a 3½-quart slow cooker and will serve 4 to 6 people. Heat settings are:

Low — 200° F
High — 300° High

Select temperature settings on your slow cooker as close as possible to the ones used here. Suggested cooking time is indicated at the top of each recipe. Unless it is recommended that a recipe be cooked only at the High setting, the cooking time listed is for the Low setting.

2

Soups and Stews

Few dishes lend themselves to the slow cooker as superbly as do soups and stews. The appliance makes their preparation so easy and convenient that soups may regain their traditional importance.

Today too often relegated to the quick-lunch category of canned soup and sandwich, soups were once such an important part of the evening meal that the French *la soupe* is the source of our word "supper."

With a slow cooker, you can toss the ingredients into the pot in the morning, leave home, and return in the evening to a light, appetite-provoking first-course soup, or a hearty meal that needs only bread and a salad as accompaniment.

The best soups are made with homemade stock, and recipes for beef and chicken stock are included here. You may want to prepare a double batch and freeze half for later use. When the soup is cooked, pour leftovers in glass jars and chill quickly in a bowl of ice water. Leave adequate air space (1″ for pint jars, 1½″ for quarts). Tightly covered, a stock should last up to two weeks in the refrigerator. If your time is limited, substitute one of the prepared stocks now available in supermarkets.

Beef Stock

Cooking time: 12 hours

- 2 pounds beef shank
- 1 pound cracked beef bones
- 1 diced celery stalk with leaves
- 4 peppercorns
- ¼ teaspoon dried marjoram
- 4 cups cold water

1. Place all ingredients in slow cooker.
2. Cover pot and cook on Low for 12 hours. If you are home, occasionally skim off scum that rises to the top.
3. Skim off scum; strain stock. Remove bones and cool. Scoop the marrow from the bones and return with meat to the stock. Omit meat if clear stock is desired.
4. Pour beef stock into jar, cover, and refrigerate.

Chicken Stock

Cooking time: 8-12 hours

- 1 chicken or chicken carcass with skin and some meat
- 1 diced celery stalk with leaves
- 2 quartered carrots
- 2 medium quartered onions
- 3 sprigs fresh parsley
- ¼ teaspoon thyme
- 4 peppercorns
- 2 teaspoons salt
- 4 cups cold water

1. Place all ingredients in slow cooker. If using whole chicken, wrap in cheesecloth to keep in good shape for later use.
2. Cover pot and cook on Low 8-12 hours.
3. Strain stock and remove bones. Return chicken meat to stock if desired. Refrigerate in covered jar. Skim off congealed fat before using.

Pale Tomato Soup

Cooking time: 8-10 hours

6 cups clear chicken broth
8 ripe whole tomatoes
1 teaspoon lemon juice
Dash of sugar
Salt to taste
3 peppercorns
¼ bay leaf
1 sprig fresh thyme
1 clove
Croutons and chopped fresh chives as garnish

1. Combine broth, tomatoes, lemon juice, sugar, salt, peppercorns, ¼ bay leaf, thyme, and clove in slow cooker.
2. Cover and cook on Low 8-10 hours.
3. Strain soup. Garnish with croutons and chopped chives.

Menu

Pale Tomato Soup
Chicken Kiev
Rice-Broccoli Ring
Dry White Wine
Raspberry Sherbet

Lentil Soup

Cooking time: 8-10 hours

2 cups lentils, washed and drained
1 ham bone with some meat on it
2 tablespoons cooking oil
2 chopped carrots
2 chopped stalks celery
1 medium sliced onion
5 cups water
1 16-ounce can of tomatoes
2 envelopes of beef broth mix
2 bay leaves
Salt and pepper to taste
1 Polish sausage (Kielbasi)
2 tablespoons red wine vinegar

1. Fry ham bone in skillet in hot oil over medium heat for a few minutes. Add carrots, celery, and onion to skillet and cook over medium heat for 15 minutes. Remove to slow cooker.
2. To slow cooker, add lentils, water, tomatoes, broth mix, bay leaves, salt, pepper, and whole sausage. Cover and cook on Low 8-10 hours. Just before serving, remove bay leaves and ham bone. Remove sausage, cut into bite-sized pieces, and return to cooker. Stir in vinegar and serve.

Menu

Lentil Soup
Rye Bread
Tossed Salad with Oil and Vinegar Dressing
Blueberry Turnovers

Black Bean Soup

Cooking time: 12-14 hours

- ½ pound black beans
- Water to cover
- 2 large chopped onions
- 2 chopped stalks celery
- 1 ham bone, or pieces of leftover ham
- 1 bay leaf
- 1 teaspoon cumin seed
- 1 clove
- Salt to taste
- ¼ teaspoon dry mustard
- 6 peppercorns
- ¼ teaspoon cayenne pepper
- 4 cups cold water

1. To beans in large kettle, add just enough water to cover. Bring to boil and cook 30 minutes. Remove from heat and soak 1½ hours. (Beans can also be soaked overnight in cold water as alternate to step 1.)
2. Drain beans and place in slow cooker with onions, celery, ham or ham bone, bay leaf, cumin seed, clove, salt, dry mustard, peppercorns and cayenne pepper. Add 4 cups water.
3. Cover and cook on High 10-12 hours.
4. Discard ham bone. Serve with a selection of garnishes, including some or all of the following: cooked rice, thin slices of lemon, sliced hard-cooked eggs, avocado slices dipped in lemon juice.

Menu

Black Bean Soup
Baked Stuffed Fish
Mixed Salad Greens
White Wine
Lemon Chiffon Pie

Minestrone

Cooking time: 7-9 hours

- 2 cups large dry white beans
- 10 cups beef bouillon
- 1 clove garlic, minced
- 1 bay leaf
- ½ cup olive oil
- 1 large, coarsely chopped onion
- 1 cup thinly sliced carrots
- 2 unpeeled, sliced zucchini
- 1 cup cut green beans
- 1 teaspoon basil
- 2 cups shredded cabbage
- 1 one-pound can tomatoes
- 1 cup broken-up spaghetti
- Salt to taste
- Freshly ground black pepper
- Grated Parmesan cheese for garnish

1. Wash beans, cover with water, and soak overnight.
2. Drain beans, return to kettle and add bouillon, garlic, and bay leaf. Bring to boil, reduce heat and simmer, covered, one hour.
3. In skillet, heat olive oil. Add onions and carrots and sauté lightly, coating with oil. Remove with slotted spoon and

drain on paper towel. Add zucchini and green beans to skillet and toss until well coated. Remove with slotted spoon and drain on paper towel.

4. Remove white beans with liquid to 4½-quart slow cooker. Add sautéed vegetables and remaining ingredients. Cover and cook on Low 6-8 hours (High 4-5 hours). Serve with cheese sprinkled over top.

Menu

Minestrone
Toasted Garlic Rounds
Salad with Vinaigrette Dressing
Cheesecake

Navy Bean Soup

Cooking time: 10-12 hours

- 1 pound navy beans
- Ham bone with some meat on it
- 8 cups water
- 3 chopped carrots
- 2 medium chopped onions
- 5 cubed potatoes
- ½ clove garlic, minced
- ⅛ teaspoon rosemary
- ⅛ teaspoon red pepper

1. Soak beans overnight. Drain and place in 4½-quart slow cooker with ham bone. Add 8 cups water and remaining ingredients.
2. Cover and cook on Low 10-12 hours. Discard ham bone before serving.

Menu

Navy Bean Soup
Hot Garlic Bread
Mixed Green Salad
Orange Cupcakes

Splendid Split Pea Soup

Cooking time: 10-12 hours

- 4 cups split peas
- 8 cups water
- 1 pound Canadian bacon cut in bite-sized pieces
- 3 large chopped onions
- 2 chopped carrots
- 6 large sprigs parsley
- ½ teaspoon celery seed
- 2 bay leaves
- ¼ teaspoon cayenne pepper
- Salt to taste
- Cheese croutons

1. Wash and drain the peas. Place in large kettle with water, bring to a boil, and boil 2 minutes. Remove from heat. Put peas, water, bacon, and remaining ingredients except croutons in 4½-quart slow cooker.
2. Cover and cook on Low 10-12 hours.
3. When cooked, whirl in a blender to purée. Return to slow cooker and reheat. Garnish with croutons.

Menu

Splendid Split Pea Soup
Corn Sticks
Red Wine
Peach Tarts

Cabbage Soup

Cooking time: 8-10 hours

4 cups chicken stock
1 small head of white cabbage
1 medium chopped onion
1 chopped carrot
Salt and pepper to taste
½ cup sour cream
1 tablespoon flour
⅛ teaspoon ground allspice
Finely chopped dill and parsley as garnish

1. Place all ingredients except dill and parsley in slow cooker.
2. Cover and cook on Low 8-10 hours.
3. Just before serving, sprinkle dill and parsley over top of soup.

Menu

Cabbage Soup
Dark Rye Bread
Cold Beer or Iced Tea
Peach Melba

Peanut Soup

Cooking time: 6-8 hours

1 cup peanut butter
⅓ cup butter
2 tablespoons diced onion
1 tablespoon diced celery

1½ tablespoons flour
1 cup evaporated milk
2 cups chicken broth
1 teaspoon salt
Freshly ground pepper
1 tablespoon lemon juice
⅓ cup unsalted peanuts, chopped

1. Melt butter in skillet. Sauté onion and celery until tender. Sprinkle with flour. Remove from heat and stir in peanut butter. Gradually stir in evaporated milk, broth, salt, pepper, and lemon juice. Place all ingredients in slow cooker.
2. Cover and cook on Low 6-8 hours. If soup seems too thick, add water. It should be the consistency of cream of tomato soup.
3. Just before serving, strain mixture and add chopped peanuts. If you have trouble finding unsalted peanuts, use chunky peanut butter.

Menu

Cup of Peanut Soup
Chicken Jambalaya
Mandarin Orange Salad
Caramel Custard

Vichyssoise

Cooking time: 12 hours

3 large chopped leeks, white part only
1 small chopped onion
2 tablespoons butter
3 large peeled and sliced potatoes
3 cups chicken broth

1 cup water
2 teaspoons salt
White pepper to taste
⅔ cup heavy cream
Finely chopped chives

(This chilled soup makes a perfect light summer meal. Cook the soup in the slow cooker overnight without heating up the kitchen. In the morning, place it in the refrigerator for a cool treat that evening.)

1. Sauté leeks and onion in butter until soft.
2. Place leeks and onion in slow cooker with potatoes, chicken broth, water, salt, and pepper.
3. Cover and cook on Low 12 hours.
4. Purée ingredients in blender. Pour into a large bowl. Chill in refrigerator until icy cold.
5. Just before serving, stir in heavy cream. Sprinkle chopped chives over top and serve immediately.

Menu

Vichyssoise
Hot Rolls
Crab and Egg Salads
Honeydew Melon

Chili Con Carne

Cooking time: 8-10 hours

2 pounds ground beef
1 medium onion
2 tablespoons bacon fat

- 2 16-ounce cans tomato wedges, drained
- 1-2 15½-ounce cans kidney beans, drained
- 1 15-ounce can tomato sauce
- 1 teaspoon salt
- ½ bay leaf
- 1-2 tablespoons chili powder

1. Sauté onion in hot fat until tender. Add ground beef and brown well.
2. Drain off fat and place meat and onions in slow cooker with tomato wedges, kidney beans, tomato sauce, and seasoning.
3. Cover and cook on Low 10-12 hours. Serves 6.

Menu

Chili Con Carne
Oyster Crackers
Fresh Fruit Plate

12-Hour Beef Stew

Cooking time: 10-12 hours

- 2½ pounds beef stew meat
- Salt and pepper
- 3 tablespoons uncooked minute tapioca
- 1 medium sliced onion
- 3 medium potatoes, sliced thick lengthwise
- 6 sliced carrots
- 2 tablespoons brown sugar
- 1 sliced stalk celery
- 1 8-ounce can tomato sauce

1. Season meat. Place in bottom of slow cooker. Sprinkle with tapioca.

2. Over meat, arrange layer of onion, then layer of potatoes, then layer of carrots. Sprinkle brown sugar over carrots. Place celery over carrots. Pour tomato sauce over top.
3. Cover and cook on Low 10-12 hours. Serves 6.

Menu

12-Hour Beef Stew
Waldorf Salad
Ice Cream Sundaes

Hearthside Beef Stew

Cooking time: 10-12 hours

2 pounds chuck roast cut in half-inch cubes
3 tablespoons vegetable oil
1 minced clove garlic
4 cups boiling water
1 teaspoon salt
1 teaspoon lemon juice
1 teaspoon sugar
1 teaspoon Worcestershire sauce
½ teaspoon pepper
½ teaspoon paprika
1 bay leaf
⅛ teaspoon allspice
6 quartered carrots
1 pound small white onions
2 large diced potatoes

1. Brown meat in hot oil in heavy skillet. Remove to slow cooker. Add remaining ingredients.
2. Cover and cook on Low 10-12 hours.
3. If stew is not as thick as you like it, stir in paste of ¼ cup flour

and ¼ cup water, turn slow cooker to High, and stir until stew reaches the thickness desired.

Menu

Hearthside Beef Stew
Mixed Fruit Salad
Spice Cake

Vegetable Beef Soup

Cooking time: 10-12 or 12-24 hours

2 pounds beef chuck or stew meat cut into cubes
1 tablespoon vegetable oil
8 cups boiling water
5 beef bouillon cubes
1 2-pound 3-ounce can Italian plum tomatoes
4 sliced carrots
4 medium diced onions
2 diced white turnips
2 teaspoons salt
½ teaspoon pepper
3 whole cloves
1 cup fresh or frozen peas
1 cup finely cut green beans
½ cup finely cut celery
1 cup uncooked elbow macaroni

1. Brown meat cubes in hot vegetable oil. Dissolve bouillon cubes in 8 cups boiling water. Add to skillet and scrape pan to pick up beef bits. Transfer meat and bouillon to slow cooker. Add all remaining ingredients except macaroni.
2. Cover and cook on Low 6-8 hours. Add macaroni and cook at least 4 more hours or until macaroni is tender. (2 medium

diced potatoes may be substituted for macaroni. If so, add with other ingredients at the beginning of cooking period and cook on Low 12-24 hours.)

Menu

Vegetable Beef Soup
Hot Bread with Herb Butter
Cherry Tarts

Blanquette of Veal

Cooking time: 4-6 hours

2	pounds veal shoulder and breast, or rump
12-15	small white peeled onions
1	peeled carrot
1	chopped celery stalk
2	cups fresh mushrooms
	Bouquet garni (2 pieces celery, 3 sprigs parsley, 1 clove, ½ bay leaf, and ¼ teaspoon dried thyme tied loosely in cheesecloth)
4	cups chicken stock or veal stock
¼	cup flour
¼	cup butter
3	beaten egg yolks
¼	cup heavy cream
2	tablespoons lemon juice

1. Cut veal into one-inch pieces. Place veal in cold salted water, bring slowly to a boil in uncovered pan and simmer for two minutes. Drain and rinse with cold water.
2. Put meat into slow cooker with onions, carrot, celery, mushrooms, and bouquet garni. Add stock.
3. Cover and cook on Low 4-6 hours.

4. Combine flour and butter and add to the pot juices. Stir well.
5. Combine beaten egg yolks and cream with 2 tablespoons of the liquid from the slow cooker. Return to pan and stir well. Just before serving, add lemon juice.

Menu

Blanquette of Veal
Buttered Noodles
Salad of Mixed Greens
Lemon Cupcakes

Brunswick Stew

Cooking time: 6-8 hours

- 1 4-pound chicken cut into serving pieces
- ¼ cup butter
- ½ cup chopped onion
- 1 1-pound 3-ounce can tomatoes
- 2 cups boiling water
- 1 8-ounce can tomato paste
- Dash of cayenne
- Salt and pepper to taste
- 3 cups corn
- 3 cups baby lima beans
- 2 tablespoons Worcestershire sauce

1. Melt butter in skillet and brown chicken well on all sides. Remove chicken to slow cooker. Add onion to skillet and cook until tender. Transfer to slow cooker.
2. Add tomatoes, water, tomato paste, cayenne, salt, and pepper to slow cooker.
3. Cover and cook on Low 4-5 hours. Skim off any fat. Add corn and lima beans.

4. Cover and cook on Low an additional 2-3 hours. (If you wish, you may remove chicken when you add the vegetables, take the meat from the bones, and return the meat to the pot.)
5. Just before serving, correct seasoning and add Worcestershire sauce.

Menu

Brunswick Stew
Corn Muffins
Molded Lime and Vegetable Salad
Peach Pie

Last-of-The-Turkey Soup

Cooking time: 12-18 hours

1 turkey carcass
2 celery stalks with leaves
1 large sliced onion
½ bay leaf
Salt and pepper to taste
Water to cover carcass
4 sliced carrots
1 large diced turnip
2 large diced potatoes
1 cup uncooked egg noodles

1. Place turkey carcass in the slow cooker with celery, onion, bay leaf, salt, and pepper. Cover carcass with cold water.
2. Cover pot and cook on Low 8-12 hours.
3. Remove bones; leave the meat. Put soup in large bowl and place in refrigerator until fat congeals on top. Skim off fat.

4. Return soup to slow cooker. Add carrots, turnip, and potatoes. Cover and cook 4-6 hours on Low.
5. Just before serving, add noodles and cook uncovered on High for another 10-12 minutes.

Menu

Last-of-the-Turkey Soup
Potato Bread
Cranberry Molded Salad
Apple Kuchen

Gulf Coast Bouillabaisse

Cooking time: 5-8 hours

1½ pounds fillet of sole, fresh or frozen
1½ pounds fillet of halibut or sea bass, fresh or frozen
1 cup raw oysters, fresh or canned
1 cup cooked crab meat
1 cup cooked shrimp
⅓ cup olive oil
½ cup chopped onion
1 minced clove garlic
3 fresh peeled and chopped tomatoes
2 tablespoons chopped parsley
1 crushed bay leaf
½ cup white wine
1½-2 cups water
1 8-ounce can tomato sauce
Pinch of saffron
¼ teaspoon thyme
Dash of Tabasco
Salt and pepper to taste

1. Heat olive oil in heavy skillet. Sauté onion, garlic, tomatoes, parsley, and bay leaf for about five minutes. Remove to slow cooker. Add wine, water, tomato sauce, and other seasonings.
2. Cover and cook on High for 2-4 hours.
3. Add seafood. Cover and cook an additional 3-4 hours on High. (You may vary types of seafood according to your tastes and local availability. Use 5-6 pounds in all. Other possibilities include lobster, sea perch, flounder, red snapper, rockfish, or mackerel.)

Menu

Gulf Coast Bouillabaisse
Salad of Mixed Greens
Hot French Bread
Lemon Cheesecake

Red Snapper Soup

Cooking time: 5-8 hours

2 pounds red snapper fillets
1 cup dry white wine
¼ cup tomato purée
¾ cup chopped tomatoes
¼ cup chopped green pepper
¼ cup chopped onion
1 chopped celery stalk
¼ clove garlic, minced
¼ teaspoon parsley flakes
Salt and pepper to taste
Pinch of thyme
Hot sauce (optional)

1. Cut fillets into half-inch pieces.
2. Combine all ingredients except fish, thyme, and hot sauce in slow cooker.
3. Cover and cook 2-4 hours on High.
4. Add fish, cover pot, and cook additional 3-4 hours on High.
5. Stir briskly until the fish flakes. Add thyme, additional salt and pepper and hot sauce to taste. May be served over rice.

Menu

Red Snapper Soup
Mixed Salad Greens
French Dressing
Hot Herb Bread
Pecan Pie

Creole Gumbo

Cooking time: 5-8 hours

2 cups canned or frozen crab meat (or 6 cleaned crabs)
2 pounds (4 cups) fresh or frozen shelled and deveined shrimp
3 diced slices bacon
2 large chopped onions
2 minced cloves garlic
2 bay leaves
1 minced green pepper
¼ teaspoon thyme
1 teaspoon salt
1 teaspoon pepper
1 package frozen okra (or 3 cups fresh, chopped)
3 tablespoons flour
4 cups chicken broth

1 16-ounce can tomatoes
Dash of Tabasco
Dash of cayenne pepper

1. Fry bacon pieces in skillet until crisp. Remove and reserve bacon. In bacon drippings, sauté onion until golden. Add garlic, bay leaves, green pepper, thyme, salt, and pepper. Cook until green pepper is slightly tender. Add okra and flour and gradually stir in chicken broth.
2. Place ingredients from skillet in slow cooker with tomatoes (including liquid), Tabasco, and cayenne pepper.
3. Cover and cook on High 2-4 hours.
4. Add crab, shrimp, and bacon pieces. Cover and cook an additional 3-4 hours on High. Serve over rice.

Menu

Creole Gumbo
French Bread
Key Lime Pie

3

Meats

Slow cooking of meat has two decided advantages for the modern cook: you can cook "Sunday" dinners any day of the week because they cook untended while you're away, and you can transform less expensive cuts of meat into tender, delicious—and yes, even exotic—company meals.

The slow cooking method softens the connective tissues of the meat to make it more tender and minimizes shrinkage. Therefore you can buy less expensive meats without sacrificing taste.

If you are not experienced in braising meats, you should take some time to discover the various cuts of meat that lend themselves to this cooking method and experiment to see how herbs, spices, and marinades can glamorize even the most humble cuts of meat. A patient and sympathetic butcher can be an invaluable ally. Don't be afraid to ask his advice. As a general rule, look for the following cuts:

Beef. Chuck, round, rump, and brisket make excellent pot roasts. Choose the least expensive or experiment to see which you like best. For braised steaks, select flank, round, or chuck steaks. Other good slow cooker cuts are short ribs and corned beef briskets.

Veal. Leg of veal, breast, shoulder, standing rump, and shank are economical cuts of veal, excellent for roasts or braised veal dishes.

Lamb. Use shoulder instead of loin chops, and leg of lamb or a rolled breast for roasts.

Pork and Ham. Use Boston butt or shoulder picnic hams, shoulder hocks and spareribs, and shoulder chops instead of the more expensive loin chops.

Sausage and variety meats. Experiment with various types of sausages, including knockwurst, chorizo (from Spain and Latin America), Italian and Polish sausages. Liver, tongue, heart, kidneys, and oxtail may also be braised successfully.

Although some slow cooker manufacturers say you don't have to brown meats before cooking in the slow cooker, I think the flavor and appearance of meats are improved by browning them first.

All meats should be cleaned and wiped well if they are put directly into the cooker. If the roast is too large to fit in your slow cooker in one piece, cut it in two.

If you are adapting recipes from other sources, you will find that less liquid is needed when cooking in the slow cooker. Use the recipes in this chapter as a guide for amount of liquid and cooking time. Since meat usually takes longer than vegetables in a slow cooker, when you cook them together, place vegetables around the bottom and sides.

To make gravy from the liquid in a slow cooker, either add 2 or 3 tablespoons of minute tapioca at the beginning so the juice thickens as it cooks, or, when the dish is cooked, mix in a paste of ¼ cup of flour or cornstarch and ¼ cup water. Turn the cooker to High and stir well. If you want to thicken the juices and reduce the liquid, remove the cover, turn the cooker to High, and cook for approximately 45 minutes.

Wrap leftovers in freezer paper and store in freezer. Most meats will keep for 2-3 months.

Simply Superb Beef Stroganoff

Cooking time: 6-8 hours

1	1½-pound round steak
	Salt and freshly ground pepper
4	tablespoons butter
1	medium sliced onion
½	clove garlic, minced
2	10½-ounce can condensed tomato soup
1	cup bouillon
	Dash of Tabasco
1	2½-ounce jar of sliced mushrooms
	Pint of sour cream

1. Cut round steak into thin strips and season with salt and pepper. Melt butter in skillet and sauté onions and garlic until soft. Remove onions and garlic. Add round steak strips and brown well over medium heat.
2. Place steak in slow cooker with onion and garlic. Stir in tomato soup, bouillon, and Tabasco.
3. Cover and cook on Low 6-8 hours. Add mushrooms 30 minutes before serving.
4. Serve stroganoff over rice with dollops (4-5 tablespoons) of sour cream on top.

Menu

Simply Superb Beef Stroganoff
Rice
Mixed Greens Salad with Oil and Vinegar Dressing
Strawberries Romanoff

Beef Rolls à la Suisse

Cooking time: 7-10 hours

3 pounds flank (or round) steak pounded thin
1 teaspoon salt
Freshly ground pepper
¼ teaspoon thyme
⅛ teaspoon nutmeg
½ cup minced ham
½ cup grated Swiss cheese
3 tablespoons chopped parsley
3 tablespoons butter
1 cup peeled chopped tomatoes
1 cup dry white wine
½ cup water
¼ pound sliced mushrooms
1 bay leaf

1. Cut steak into 12 rectangular pieces. Season one side of each piece with salt, pepper, thyme, and nutmeg. On the opposite side place a mixture of ham, cheese, and parsley. Beginning with the short side, roll the steak tightly around the mixture and tie with thread or fasten with toothpick.
2. Melt butter in skillet and brown rolls on all sides. Place in slow cooker. Add tomatoes, wine, water, mushrooms, and bay leaf.
3. Cover and cook on Low 7-10 hours.
4. Discard bay leaf, thicken sauce if desired, and serve over meat.

Menu

Beef Rolls à la Suisse
Green Beans and Cauliflower
French Tomato Salad
Peach Melba

Danish Beef Rolls

Cooking time: 7-10 hours

2 pounds round (or flank) steak pounded thin
1 large diced yellow onion
4 medium sliced dill pickles
4 quartered slices bacon
½ cup mushroom slices
2 tablespoons vegetable oil
1 cup water
1 bouillon cube
⅛ teaspoon thyme
Salt and pepper to taste

1. Cut round steak into 12-16 rectangular pieces. On each piece place a little onion, 1 slice dill pickle, 1 piece bacon, and several mushrooms. Beginning with the short side, roll each piece and fasten with toothpicks or thread.
2. Brown rolls in oil on all sides and add to slow cooker.
3. Add water to bouillon cube, let dissolve, then add to pot. Add thyme, salt, and pepper.
4. Cover and cook on Low 7-10 hours.

Menu

Danish Beef Rolls
Oven-Browned Potatoes
Spinach Soufflé
Danish Pastries

Steak Roll Parmesan

Cooking time: 7-10 hours

- 2-3 pounds flank (or round) steak pounded thin
- 1 small can mushroom pieces
- 1 small diced onion
- 4 tablespoons (grated) Parmesan cheese
- Salt and pepper to taste
- 1 tablespoon parsley flakes
- 3 tablespoons vegetable oil
- 1½ cups beef bouillon
- ¼ cup flour
- ¼ cup water

1. Place mushrooms, onion, cheese, salt, pepper, and parsley along center of steak. Beginning with short side, roll as tightly as possible into one large roll. Fasten with string. Brown meat roll well on all sides in hot oil in skillet. Place in slow cooker and add bouillon.
2. Cover and cook on Low 7-10 hours (on High 3-4 hours).
3. Thicken cooking liquid with mixture of ¼ cup flour and ¼ cup water or tiny pellets of butter and flour. Place roll on serving platter and pour gravy over it.

Menu

Steak Roll Parmesan
Buttered Green Noodles
Carrots Vichy
Spumoni and Sugar Cookies

Pepper Steak

Cooking time: 8 hours

- 1 pound round steak cut into thin strips
- 1 clove garlic
- ½ cup sliced onion

4 tablespoons butter or margarine
Salt and pepper
2 medium sliced green peppers
½ pound sliced mushrooms
3 quartered tomatoes
½ cup red wine
Cornstarch

1. Sauté garlic and onion in melted butter for a few minutes. Remove garlic and onion and add round steak strips seasoned with salt and pepper to taste. Brown meat.
2. Remove meat and place in slow cooker. Sauté green pepper and mushrooms in butter for five minutes. Add tomatoes, cook about a minute, then season with salt and pepper and add to slow cooker.
3. Add onions and wine to slow cooker. Discard garlic.
4. Cover and cook on Low until tender, approximately 8 hours.
5. Thicken liquid in pot with cornstarch until sauce consistency. Serve over rice.

Menu

Pepper Steak
Rice
Mandarin Orange Salad
Raspberry Sherbet

Savory Steak

Cooking time: 9 hours

2 pounds round steak cut into strips
¼ cup olive oil
⅛ cup red wine vinegar

- ½ cup hot water
- 1½ tablespoons grated onion
- 1 tablespoon steak sauce
- 1 tablespoon chili sauce
- ½ clove garlic, grated
- 2 teaspoons brown sugar
- ½ teaspoon salt
- ½ teaspoon dry mustard
- ¼ teaspoon pepper

1. Brown steak in olive oil; place in slow cooker. Combine remaining ingredients and pour over steak.
2. Cover and cook on High 1 hour. Turn to Low and cook another 8 hours. Serve with rice.

Menu

Savory Steak
Rice
Fried Zucchini
Lemon Cheesecake

Swiss Steak

Cooking time: 9-11 hours

- 1 ¾-inch-thick round steak cut in serving pieces (about 2 pounds)
- 1 teaspoon salt
- Freshly ground pepper
- 1 finely chopped clove garlic
- ¼ cup flour
- 3 tablespoons vegetable oil
- 1 medium sliced onion
- 1 green pepper, cut in rings

- 1 6-ounce can tomato paste
- 1 16-ounce can tomatoes, undrained
- ½ teaspoon basil
- 1 bay leaf
- ½ teaspoon sugar
- ¼ teaspoon vinegar

1. Season steak with salt and pepper. Rub with garlic. Dredge in flour and brown well in hot oil in skillet.
2. Add to slow cooker with remaining ingredients. Cover and cook on High 1 hour; turn to Low and cook an additional 8-10 hours.

Menu

Swiss Steak
Buttered Noodles
Green Beans and Almonds
Mixed Fruit Salad
Blueberry Cobbler

Round Steak Beer Simmer

Cooking time: 8-10 hours

- 2 pounds of top round steak
- ¾ teaspoon salt
- ¼ teaspoon pepper
- 3 tablespoons flour
- 3 tablespoons butter or margarine
- 1 crushed clove garlic
- 1 large thinly sliced onion
- 1 cup beer
- ½ cup water
- 1 sprig parsley

1 sprig thyme
1 stalk celery cut in 3-4 pieces
1 bay leaf
1 4-ounce can mushrooms (optional)

1. Mix salt, pepper, and 2 tablespoons flour and pound it into the meat.
2. Brown meat quickly on high temperature in 1 tablespoon butter or margarine in skillet. Remove meat to slow cooker.
3. Add remaining butter or margarine to skillet and lightly sauté garlic and onion. Stir in beer and water and bring to a boil. Pour over meat in the slow cooker. Add mushrooms and seasonings.
4. Cook covered on Low 8-10 hours.
5. Remove meat; turn slow cooker to High. Thicken sauce with about 1 tablespoon flour. Pour over meat and serve.

Menu

Round Steak Beer Simmer
Creamed Potato Casserole
Asparagus
Boston Cream Pie

Forester Casserole

Cooking time: 8-10 hours

1½-2 pounds round steak cut into one-inch cubes
6 tablespoons butter
2 medium sliced onions
1 cup beef bouillon
1¼ teaspoons salt
½ teaspoon freshly ground black pepper
¼ teaspoon nutmeg

2 medium potatoes (2-3 cups), sliced very thin
2 cups thinly sliced cooking apples
2 tablespoons dry bread crumbs

(Leftover pot roast cut into cubes may be subsituted for round steak.)

1. Melt 3 tablespoons butter in skillet and sauté onions until golden. Remove onions, add meat to skillet, and brown well over high heat. Add bouillon, salt, pepper, and nutmeg and stir.
2. In bottom of slow cooker arrange half the potatoes. Add, in order, layer of meat mixture, onions, apples. Top with another layer of potatoes. Sprinkle with bread crumbs and dot with rest of butter.
3. Cover and cook on Low 8-10 hours (4 hours on High).

Menu

Forester Casserole
Brussels Sprouts
Avocado Salad
Lime Sherbet

Home-Style Pot Roast

Cooking time: 10-12 hours

1 3-4-pound chuck roast
1 large quartered onion
8-12 large carrots, split lengthwise
4-6 quartered potatoes
Flour
3 tablespoons butter or margarine

½ cup bouillon
Salt and pepper to taste

1. Peel onion, carrots, and potatoes and cut up as directed. Place in bottom of slow cooker.
2. Dredge pot roast with flour. Melt butter and brown pot roast on both sides over medium heat in skillet.
3. Place pot roast on top of vegetables. Add bouillon, salt, and pepper.
4. Cover and cook on Low 10-12 hours.

Menu

Home-Style Pot Roast
Potatoes, Onions, and Carrots
Hot Rolls
Tossed Salad with Green Goddess Dressing
Peach Turnovers

Mushroom Pot Roast

Cooking time: 10-12 hours

1 4-pound pot roast
Flour
Cooking oil
Salt and pepper
2 cups sliced onions
¼ cup water
¼ cup catsup
¼ cup dry sherry
1 minced clove garlic
¼ teaspoon each dry mustard, marjoram, rosemary, and thyme

1 medium crushed bay leaf
1 cup (8-ounce can) sliced mushrooms, drained
¼ cup water
¼ cup flour

1. Trim excess fat from meat. (Cut in half to fit 3½-quart slow cooker.) Dredge meat in a small amount of flour. Brown meat in skillet in hot oil. Sprinkle with salt and pepper. Remove roast and place in slow cooker. Cover with onions.
2. Stir together water, catsup, sherry, garlic, and seasonings. Pour over pot roast.
3. Cover and cook on Low 10-12 hours.
4. Remove meat. Skim excess fat from sauce. Add mushrooms. Stir ¼ cup water into ¼ cup flour; then gradually stir into juices in pot. Cook on High, stirring constantly, until gravy thickens and boils. Serve gravy over pot roast.

Menu

Mushroom Pot Roast
Boiled New Potatoes
Grilled Tomatoes
Peas and Onions
Chocolate Soufflé

Caraway Pot Roast

Cooking time: 10-12 hours

4 pounds pot roast
¼ cup flour
3 teaspoons salt
Freshly ground black pepper
2 tablespoons vegetable oil

2 large sliced onions
1 tablespoon paprika
3 teaspoons caraway seeds
1 8-ounce can tomato sauce
½ cup water

1. Dredge pot roast with flour and season with salt and pepper. Brown roast and onions in hot oil over medium heat.
2. Place onions and pot roast in slow cooker. Add remaining ingredients.
3. Cook covered on Low 10-12 hours.

Menu

Caraway Pot Roast
Buttered Noodles
Green Beans and Almonds
German Chocolate Cake

Cantonese Pot Roast

Cooking time: 10-12 hours

1 3-5-pound pot roast
2 tablespoons cooking oil
4 medium-sized sweet potatoes, cut in half lengthwise
½ cup brown sugar, packed
½ teaspoon salt
¼ teaspoon pepper
½ cup vinegar
¼ cup soy sauce
½ bay leaf, crumbled
2 celery stalks cut in half
1 8-ounce can water chestnuts

1. In skillet in hot oil brown pot roast well on all sides. Place roast in slow cooker, arrange sweet potatoes around edges of cooker, and add remaining ingredients except water chestnuts.
2. Cover and cook on Low 10-12 hours.
3. Add water chestnuts one hour before serving. Thicken sauce for gravy if desired.

Menu

Cantonese Pot Roast
Chinese Pea Pods
Fried Rice
Almond Cookies

Lemon Pot Roast

Cooking time: 10-12 hours

1	4-pound chuck roast
1	6-ounce can frozen lemonade concentrate
¾	cup white wine
2	slices onion
1	bay leaf
4-5	peppercorns
1	teaspoon salt
1	teaspoon cinnamon
3	cloves
1	cup sour cream (optional)

1. Combine lemonade concentrate, wine, onion, bay leaf, peppercorns, salt, cinnamon, and cloves to make a marinade. Place pot roast in large bowl and pour marinade over it. Cover and marinate for 12 hours or more.

2. Remove pot roast and save marinade. Brown roast in skillet. Place in slow cooker. Pour marinade over top.
3. Cover and cook 10-12 hours on Low.
4. For a rich sauce, just before serving, stir sour cream into cooking liquid until of gravy consistency, or substitute flour and water paste for sour cream.

Menu

Lemon Pot Roast
Fresh Fruit Kabobs
Mashed Potatoes
Lima Beans
Apple Strudel

Roast Orientale

Cooking Time: 10-12 hours

- 1 3-4 pound chuck roast
- 1 cup vinegar
- 1 slivered garlic clove
- 1 medium quartered onion
- Cooking oil
- ½ cup coffee
- ¼ cup water
- Salt and pepper to taste

1. Make several shallow slits across top of beef and place in bowl. Pour vinegar over beef. Place garlic and onion on top. Refrigerate 24 to 48 hours. Drain off vinegar and discard.
2. Brown roast on both sides in cooking oil. Add salt and pepper. Place in slow cooker. Pour coffee and water over roast.

3. Cover and cook on Low 10-12 hours.

Menu

Roast Orientale
Wild Rice Casserole
Carmelized Carrots
Tossed Salad with Roquefort Dressing
Lemon Cheesecake

Leftover Beef Casserole

Cooking time: 10-12 hours

4 cups leftover pot roast cut in half-inch cubes
2 cans condensed green pea soup
½ cup evaporated milk
¾ cup sliced mushrooms sautéed in 1 teaspoon butter
½ cup water
2 sliced carrots
½ teaspoon dried sweet basil
1 medium chopped onion
Salt and pepper to taste
2 cups fresh hot mashed potatoes
2 sprigs parsley
1 beaten egg
2 tablespoons melted butter

1. Heat soup in a pan and stir in evaporated milk.
2. Place meat, soup, mushrooms, carrots, water, basil, and onion in slow cooker. Season to taste.
3. Cover and cook on Low 8-10 hours.

4. Add parsley and beaten egg to mashed potatoes. Spread evenly over top of casserole. Drizzle melted butter over top. Turn slow cooker on High. Cook another 2 hours.

Menu

Leftover Beef Casserole
French Tomato Salad
Peppermint Ice Cream
Sugar Cookies

Darlene's Barbecued Beef Sandwiches

ooking time: 11-13 hours

- 1 4-pound pot roast
- 1 can tomato sauce
- 1 small bottle catsup
- 1 cup water
- 2 tablespoons lemon juice
- 2 teaspoons Worcestershire sauce
- 2 teaspoons brown sugar
- ½ teaspoon dry mustard
- 1 medium chopped onion
- ½ cup chopped celery
- Salt and pepper to taste

1. Place meat in slow cooker and cook on Low 10-12 hours or until tender.
2. Remove fat and bone. Shred meat. Combine remaining ingredients, add to meat in slow cooker, and simmer for one hour on Low. Makes 20 sandwiches or buns. Leftovers freeze well.

Menu

Darlene's Barbecued Beef Sandwiches
French Fries
Cole Slaw
Blond Brownies

Hamburger Stroganoff

Cooking time: 6-8 hours

- 2 pounds ground beef
- ¼ cup butter
- 2 medium chopped onions
- 2 chopped cloves garlic
- 1 16-ounce can sliced mushrooms
- 1 tablespoon flour
- 1 8-ounce can tomato sauce
- 1 cup red wine
- 1 cup beef bouillon
- 2½ teaspoons salt
- ¼ teaspoon pepper
- 1½ cups sour cream
- ½ cup grated Parmesan cheese

1. Melt butter in skillet and sauté onion, garlic, and mushrooms, until onion is golden. Add ground beef and brown well. Remove to slow cooker.
2. To slow cooker add flour, tomato sauce, wine, bouillon, salt, pepper, and sour cream. Stir well. Sprinkle with cheese.
3. Cover and cook on Low 6-8 hours.

Menu

Hamburger Stroganoff
Noodles
Whipped Gelatin Fruit Salad
Cherry Pie

Cassoulet

Cooking time: 8-10 hours

1 16-ounce package navy beans
1 pound ground beef
1 pound ground pork
1 10¾-ounce can condensed chicken broth
½ bay leaf
¼ teaspoon dried sweet basil
¼ teaspoon marjoram
2 teaspoons salt
Freshly ground pepper
4 cups water
2 medium onions
2 tablespoons salad oil
1 cup diced carrots
½ garlic clove, crushed
1 teaspoon celery flakes
1 cup water
2 slices fresh bread crumbs
1 15-ounce can tomato sauce

1. Rinse beans, discarding any stones or shriveled beans. Place beans in large saucepan with chicken broth, ½ bay leaf, basil,

marjoram, 1 teaspoon salt, pepper, and 4 cups water. Heat to boiling and boil 3 minutes. Remove from heat, cover, and let stand one hour.
2. Chop one onion; then in hot oil in skillet sauté it with carrots, celery, and garlic until lightly browned. Remove to slow cooker. Add presoaked beans with liquid. Stir well.
3. Mince remaining onion. In large bowl, mix onion with ground beef, ground pork, bread crumbs, 1 cup water, remaining teaspoon salt and pepper. Shape meat mixture into small meatballs about one inch in diameter. Brown meatballs well on all sides in skillet over medium-high heat. Place meatballs in slow cooker. Pour tomato sauce over top of casserole and stir ingredients together well.
4. Cover and cook on Low 8-10 hours.

Menu

Cassoulet
Salad of Mixed Greens
Lemon Chiffon Pie

Stuffed Cabbage Rolls

Cooking time: 6-8 hours

1 medium head cabbage
1 tablespoon butter or margarine
¼ cup minced onion
¼ pound bulk pork sausage
1 cup ground beef
2 tablespoons bread crumbs
1 cup rice, cooked
½ teaspoon salt
Freshly ground pepper
1 clove garlic

1 beaten egg
1 diced carrot
1 diced onion
2 bacon slices
1 16-ounce can tomatoes

1. Cook rice according to package directions. Bring kettle of salted water to a boil, and simmer cabbage head five minutes. Plunge cabbage into cold water and roll in towel to dry.
2. Melt butter in skillet and sauté onion until soft. Add sausage and ground beef and brown well. Drain excess fat, remove from heat, and add bread crumbs, rice, salt, pepper, garlic, and egg. Mix well.
3. Arrange carrots and onion in bottom of slow cooker. Lay two lengths of string to form an x on top of vegetables. The string should be long enough to tie around cabbage. Place whole cabbage on top of string, stem end down. With a sharp knife remove a core approximately 3 inches in diameter from center of cabbage. Do not cut any deeper than about 2 inches from bottom of cabbage. Fill the cavity with stuffing mixture from the skillet. Place bacon slices over the top and tie cabbage with string to hold leaves around stuffing. Pour tomatoes with juice into the slow cooker.
4. Cover and cook on Low 6-8 hours.
5. To serve, place cabbage on platter, cut string, and arrange carrots and onions around it.

Menu

Stuffed Cabbage Rolls
Mixed Fruit Salad
Coconut Cream Pie

Apple Meatballs

Cooking time: 4-6 hours

1 pound ground beef
½ cup soft bread crumbs
¼ cup water
1 medium peeled and chopped apple
2 tablespoons chopped onion
2 tablespoons butter or margarine
1 egg
1 teaspoon salt
Freshly ground pepper
1 teaspoon horseradish
Flour
Cooking oil
1 10½-ounce can condensed consommé

1. Mix bread crumbs with water. Set aside.
2. Sauté apple and onion in melted butter until onion is yellow. Add apples and onions to the crumbs. Add meat, egg, salt, pepper, and horseradish and mix well. Shape into small balls; roll in flour.
3. Brown meatballs on all sides. Drain and place in slow cooker. Pour consommé over meatballs.
4. Cover and cook on Low 4-6 hours (High 1½-2½ hours.)

Menu

Apple Meatballs
Buttered Noodles
Cucumber and Tomato Gelatin Salad
Green Beans and Almonds
Pumpkin Cake

Cheddar Meat Loaf

Cooking time: 9-10 hours

- 2 pounds ground beef
- 2 slightly beaten eggs
- ¼ cup chili sauce
- 2 teaspoons salt
- ½ teaspoon dry mustard
- 1 4-ounce can mushroom pieces, drained
- 1 medium finely chopped onion
- ¾ cup grated Cheddar cheese
- ⅛ teaspoon pepper

1. Mix together ground beef, eggs, chili sauce, salt, and mustard. Shape half of meat mixture into a large round patty in bottom of slow cooker.
2. Mix together well the mushrooms, onion, cheese, and pepper. Spread on top of meat in cooker. Make another large patty with remaining meat mixture and place on top of first patty.
3. Cover and cook on High 1 hour; turn to Low and cook another 8-9 hours.

Menu

Cheddar Meat Loaf
Buttered Broccoli
Soufflé Fruit Salad
Brownies and Ice Cream

Gala Meat Loaf

Cooking time: 9-10 hours

1½	pounds ground beef
1	cup bread crumbs
1	small finely chopped onion
1	slightly beaten egg
¼	cup finely diced, peeled apples
1½	teaspoons Worcestershire sauce
¼	teaspoon pepper
1½	teaspoons salt
¾	cup brown sugar
1	teaspoon dry mustard

1. Combine all ingredients except brown sugar and dry mustard. Mix well. Shape into loaf.
2. Combine brown sugar and dry mustard and spread over top. Place in slow cooker.
3. Cover and cook on High for 1 hour; turn to Low and cook another 8-9 hours.

(If you want to freeze leftovers, shape into 2 or 3 smaller loaves.)

Menu

Gala Meat Loaf
Succotash
Orange and Onion Salad
Banana Cake

New England Dinner

Cooking time: 12-24 hours

1 3-5 pound corned beef brisket
2 cups water
4 small carrots
3 small peeled and halved potatoes
3 small peeled and quartered white turnips
1 trimmed and cleaned leek
2 sprigs parsley
1 bay leaf
1 head cabbage, cut in wedges

1. Rinse corned beef to remove surface salt. Place in slow cooker. Add water, carrots, potatoes, and turnips to pot.
2. Cut a slit in the leek halfway down. Place the parsley and bay leaf in the slit and tie the leek together with a string. Add to the slow cooker.
3. Cover and cook on Low 12-24 hours. (High 7-10 hours.) After 5 or 6 hours of cooking (2-3 hours on High) add cabbage wedges to pot and stir all ingredients together. Cook remainder of time. Remove leek before serving.

(If leek is not available, tie parsley and bay leaf in cheesecloth and add to pot. Add one medium onion to pot with carrots and corned beef.)

Menu

New England Dinner
Hot Mustard, Grated Horseradish as garnishes
Beets
Potato Bread
Ginger Cookies

Beef Liver in Wine

Cooking time: 6-8 hours

- 2 pounds beef liver
- 2 tablespoons butter
- 2 tablespoons flour
- ½ cup water
- ½ cup white wine
- 2 cloves
- 1 bay leaf
- ¾ teaspoon salt
- ½ teaspoon pepper
- 12 small whole onions
- 8 diced carrots
- Parsley sprigs

1. Melt butter in skillet and brown liver well. Place in slow cooker. Stir flour into pan drippings, add water and wine. Transfer sauce to slow cooker. Add remaining ingredients except parsley.
2. Cover and cook on Low 6-8 hours.
3. Strain gravy, serve over liver, and top with parsley sprigs.

Menu

Beef Liver in Wine
Sautéed Potatoes
Baby Green Peas
Salad of Mixed Greens
Peppermint Ice Cream

Veal Stroganoff

Cooking time: 6-8 hours

- 1½-2 pounds veal cutlets pounded thin
- ¼ cup flour
- 1½ teaspoons salt

¼ teaspoon freshly ground pepper
4 tablespoons butter
1 small sliced onion
1 small can sliced mushrooms
½ cup dry white wine
½ bay leaf
1 cup sour cream

1. Slice veal cutlets in thin strips, and toss lightly in mixture of flour, salt, and pepper. Sauté veal, onions, and mushrooms in melted butter over medium heat. Place in slow cooker with wine and bay leaf.
2. Cover and cook on Low 6-8 hours. Stir in sour cream during last half hour. Serve over rice.

Menu

Veal Stroganoff
Buttered Noodles
Tossed Salad with Garnish of Beets
Almond Strudel

Veal Scallopini

Cooking time: 6-8 hours

1 2-pound veal shoulder, thinly sliced
½ cup flour
1½ teaspoons salt
½ teaspoon white pepper
½ cup minced onion
¼ cup olive oil
1 minced clove garlic
⅔ cup chicken broth
⅓ cup dry white wine
½ cup peeled, diced tomatoes
½ teaspoon rosemary
2 tablespoons Parmesan cheese
1 teaspoon sugar

1. Roll veal lightly in flour, salt, and pepper mixture. Sauté onion in hot oil in skillet until tender. Remove. Sauté veal strips in remaining oil until golden brown. Place onions, veal, and remaining ingredients into slow cooker.
2. Cover and cook on Low 6-8 hours. Serve with rice or fettucini.

Menu

Veal Scallopini
Fettucini
Caesar Salad
Coconut Macaroons

Veal Roast

Cooking time: 8-10 hours

1 4½-5-pound veal rump with bone
2 teaspoons salt
½ teaspoon pepper
2 tablespoons butter or margarine
1 bouillon cube
½ cup boiling water
2 sliced carrots
2 sliced onions
⅛ teaspoon thyme
1 bay leaf
¼ cup flour
¼ cup cold water
¾ cup cream

1. Season veal, melt butter in skillet, and brown veal well on all sides.
2. Dissolve bouillon cube in boiling water while roast is

browning. Place carrots, onions, thyme, and bay leaf in slow cooker. Place roast on top. Pour bouillon over all.

3. Cover and cook on Low 8-10 hours.
4. Remove roast when cooked. Combine flour, cream, and water and stir over Low heat until gravy is thick and smooth.

Menu

Veal Roast
Salad of Wilted Greens
Casseroled Green Beans
Riced Potatoes
Strawberry Bavarian

Veal Casserole

Cooking time: 6-8 hours

12 veal scallops
1½ pounds zucchini
2 teaspoons salt
Freshly ground pepper
¼ teaspoon nutmeg
1 cup grated Parmesan cheese
4 tablespoons butter
½ cup dry bread crumbs

1. Clean and slice zucchini. Place a third of the zucchini in bottom of slow cooker. Sprinkle with 1 teaspoon salt, pepper, and ⅛ teaspoon nutmeg.
2. Place 6 veal scallops on top of zucchini, followed by ⅓ cup of cheese. Dot with 1 tablespoon butter.
3. Arrange another layer of zucchini and season as in step 1.
4. Add remaining veal followed by ⅓ cup of cheese. Dot with 1 tablespoon butter.

5. Top the casserole with the remaining zucchini. Add remaining cheese and butter. Sprinkle on bread crumbs.
6. Cover and cook on Low 6-8 hours. Remove cover last hour.

Menu

Veal Casserole
Tossed Green Salad
Pears in White Wine

Hot Pot Casserole

Cooking time: 8-10 hours

- 2½ pounds shoulder of lamb cut into one-inch cubes
- 2 tablespoons butter or margarine
- 2 pounds thinly sliced potatoes
- 2 large sliced onions
- 5-6 medium sliced carrots
- 1 pound fresh string beans cut in half lengthwise
- 1 pound fresh sliced mushrooms
- 3 tablespoons flour
- 2 teaspoons salt
- Freshly ground pepper
- 2 cups water
- 2 beef bouillon cubes
- ¼ cup chopped parsley
- ¼ teaspoon thyme

1. Melt butter or margarine in skillet; brown lamb over medium heat.
2. Place potatoes in bottom of buttered slow cooker. Add in layers: onions, carrots, beans, lamb, mushrooms.
3. To pan drippings, add flour, salt, pepper, water, bouillon

cubes, parsley, and thyme. Cook over low heat until cubes have dissolved and sauce is thick and smooth. Pour over casserole in slow cooker.

4. Cover and cook on Low 8-10 hours.

Menu

Hot Pot Casserole
Mixed Greens
Fresh Fruit

French Bean Casserole

Cooking time: 11 hours (includes bean preparation)

½ pound dried marrow or Great Northern beans
2 cups water
1 large chopped onion
1½ teaspoons salt
½ pound cubed lamb shoulder
1 tablespoon olive oil
1 minced clove garlic
½ cup dry vermouth
1 teaspoon instant beef broth
1 teaspoon leaf thyme, crumbled
¼ teaspoon pepper
½ bay leaf

1. Rinse beans under running water. Combine beans, water, onion, and salt in large kettle. Bring to boil; cover and boil 30 minutes. Remove from heat and let stand 1½ hours.
2. Brown lamb cubes in olive oil in large skillet. Remove lamb; sauté garlic for 3 minutes. Stir in lamb cubes, vermouth, instant broth, thyme, pepper, and bay and bring to boil.

3. Drain beans, reserving liquid. Combine beans, lamb, and sauce from skillet in slow cooker. Add 1 cup liquid from bean pot.
4. Cover and cook on High one hour; turn to Low and cook another 8 hours.

Menu

French Bean Casserole
Grilled Tomatoes
Mixed Greens with Oil and Vinegar Dressing
Raspberry Tarts

Braised Shoulder of Lamb

Cooking time: 10-12 hours

1 4-5-pound shoulder of lamb, boned, rolled, and tied
2 cloves garlic, cut in slivers
2 teaspoons salt
½ teaspoon pepper
3 tablespoons olive oil
3 medium chopped onions
1 1-pound 12-ounce can tomatoes, drained
1 cup beef broth
1 teaspoon oregano
1 tablespoon minced parsley

1. Cut a few slits in lamb and insert garlic. Rub lamb with salt and pepper. Heat olive oil in heavy skillet and brown onions and lamb well.
2. Place lamb in slow cooker. Add tomatoes, broth, and oregano.
3. Cover and cook on Low 10-12 hours. Serve with pot liquid as sauce and garnish with parsley.

Menu

Braised Shoulder of Lamb
Endive Salad
Zucchini Boats
Boiled New Potatoes
Butter Pecan Ice Cream

Honey Spareribs

Cooking time: 6-8 hours

- 4 pounds spareribs cut in 3-rib sections
- 1 12-ounce can beer
- 1½ tablespoons lemon juice
- ½ cup honey
- ½ teaspoon dry mustard
- 1½ teaspoons salt
- 4 tablespoons vegetable oil

1. Place spareribs in baking dish. Mix together remaining ingredients except vegetable oil and pour over ribs. Marinate for 24 hours in refrigerator, turning frequently.
2. Remove spareribs from marinade (reserving marinade) and brown in hot oil in skillet for 30 minutes. Place in slow cooker with 1 cup marinade.
3. Cover and cook on Low 6-8 hours. To serve, pour sauce from pot over ribs.

Menu

Honey Spareribs
Chinese Fried Rice
Pea Pods
Fruit Fritters

Saucy Spareribs

Cooking time: 8½-10½ hours

- 4 pounds spareribs cut in 3-rib sections
- ⅓ cup butter or margarine, melted
- 1 small quartered onion
- 1 quartered clove garlic
- ¼ cup raisins
- 1 cup catsup
- ½ cup red wine
- 3 tablespoons brown sugar
- 2 tablespoons vinegar
- 1 tablespoon lemon juice
- 1 teaspoon dry mustard
- 1 teaspoon salt
- ¼ teaspoon each basil, black pepper, tarragon, rosemary, thyme, and marjoram

1. Put butter in slow cooker, cover, and turn to Low. Meanwhile parboil spareribs 30 minutes.
2. Place onion, garlic, and raisins in blender. Grind finely. Add remaining ingredients. Blend well. Pour into slow cooker.
3. Place spareribs in slow cooker. Coat with sauce.
4. Cover and cook on Low 8-10 hours.

Menu

Saucy Spareribs
Corn on the Cob
Cole Slaw
Blueberry Pie

Spareribs and Sauerkraut

Cooking time: 6-8 hours

- 4 pounds spareribs cut in 3-rib sections
- Butter or margarine
- Salt and pepper

1½ quarts sauerkraut
1 small sliced onion
6 small white potatoes, peeled and cut in half
1 teaspoon caraway seeds
½ cup water

1. Parboil spareribs in large kettle 3-4 minutes. Melt a small amount of butter in skillet, brown ribs over medium heat 30 minutes.
2. Salt and pepper ribs. Place sauerkraut in bottom of slow cooker. Place onion slices on top of sauerkraut. Add ribs and place potatoes around edge of pot. Add water and caraway seeds.
3. Cover and cook on Low 6-8 hours.

Menu

Spareribs and Sauerkraut
Baked Potato
Beet Salad
Apple Crunch

Braised Short Ribs

Cooking time: 7-10 hours

3-4 pounds beef short ribs
2 diced slices bacon
2 medium chopped onions
Salt and pepper to taste
2 tablespoons caraway seeds
¼ cup wine vinegar
1 cup hot water

1. Cut excess fat from ribs. In a skillet fry bacon until it begins to brown. Add onions and short ribs and cook on medium heat 15 minutes. Put onions and browned ribs in slow cooker. Add remaining ingredients.

2. Cover pot, and cook on Low 7-10 hours. Skim off any fat that rises to top of pot.

Menu

Braised Short Ribs
Scalloped Onions with Cheese
Glazed Beets
Tossed Salad with Vinegar and Oil Herb Dressing
Lemon and Orange Cupcakes

Spicy Southern Short Ribs

Cooking time: 7-10 hours

2 pounds beef short ribs
3 tablespoons cooking oil
1 medium sliced onion
2 tablespoons butter or margarine
2 tablespoons cider vinegar
½ cup tomato sauce
1 tablespoon brown sugar
1 tablespoon Worcestershire sauce
1 teaspoon mustard
½ cup water
1 teaspoon salt
⅛ teaspoon pepper

1. Sauté onion in hot oil in skillet until tender. Remove onion to a bowl and brown the ribs in skillet. Drain fat, remove ribs from pan, and place in slow cooker.
2. Combine remaining ingredients with onion to make a sauce. Pour sauce over ribs.
3. Cover and cook on Low 7-10 hours (High 4-6 hours).

Menu

Spicy Southern Short Ribs
Steamed Rice
Molded Avocado Salad
Chocolate Sundaes

Short Ribs Ranchero

Cooking time: 7-10 hours

- 3-4 pounds lean short ribs
- 3 tablespoons cooking oil
- 1 sliced lemon
- 1 large thinly sliced onion
- ⅓ cup Worcestershire sauce
- 1 cup catsup
- 1 teaspoon chili powder
- 1 teaspoon salt
- 2 dashes Tabasco
- ½ teaspoon thyme
- 1 bay leaf
- 2 cups water

1. Brown short ribs in oil in skillet. Place ribs in slow cooker.
2. Mix remaining ingredients together. Pour over short ribs.
3. Cover and cook on Low 7-10 hours.

Menu

Short Ribs Ranchero
Potato Salad
Three-Bean Salad
Sliced Tomatoes
Apple Pie

Country Pork Chops

Cooking time: 6-8 hours

4 loin pork chops
3 tablespoons cooking oil
½ teaspoon salt
¼ teaspoon pepper
½ cup flour
3-4 boiling potatoes, thinly sliced
2 medium sliced onions
1½ cups sour cream
¼ teaspoon dry mustard

1. Mix flour, salt, and pepper in bag. Shake pork chops in bag one at a time to coat. Brown in skillet in hot oil over medium heat.
2. Place potatoes in bottom of slow cooker. Follow with layer of onion rings, then layer of pork chops. Mix sour cream and mustard and spoon over top.
3. Cover and cook on Low 6-8 hours.

Menu

Country Pork Chops
Beets in Orange Sauce
Spinach Salad
Black Walnut Pie

Peachy Pork Chops

Cooking time: 6-8 hours

4-6 loin pork chops
3 tablespoons cooking oil
½ teaspoon salt
Freshly ground pepper

1 1-pound can peach halves
⅓ cup brown sugar
1½ teaspoons cinammon
⅛ teaspoon ground cloves
1 10-ounce can tomato sauce
¼ cup vinegar

1. Season chops with salt and pepper; brown well on both sides in hot cooking oil.
2. Place pork chops in bottom of slow cooker. On each chop place peach half. Reserve peach syrup.
3. Mix ¼ cup peach syrup with sugar, cinnamon, cloves, and tomato sauce. Pour over chops and peaches.
4. Cover and cook on Low 6-8 hours until tender.
5. Remove pork chops, stir in vinegar, and serve sauce over chops.

Menu

Peachy Pork Chops
Scalloped Potatoes
Broccoli
Tossed Salad with Oil and Vinegar Dressing
Chocolate Chip Cookies

Pork Chop Casserole

Cooking time: 3½ hours

4-6 loin pork chops
Salt and pepper
3 tablespoons cooking oil
4-6 tablespoons uncooked minute rice
4-6 slices onion
1 1-pound can tomato halves

1. Season pork chops and brown in hot oil over medium heat.
2. Place chops in bottom of slow cooker. On each chop, place onion slice, 1 tablespoon rice, and tomato half, inverted. Pour juice from tomato can into pot.
3. Cover and cook on High approximately 3½ hours or until chops are tender and rice is cooked.

Menu

Pork Chop Casserole
Snap Green Beans
Mixed Green Salad with Russian Dressing
Peach Pie

Orangeberry Pork Chops

Cooking time: 6-8 hours

4 thick pork chops
Salt and freshly ground pepper
3 tablespoons bacon fat
2 large oranges
2 tablespoons brown sugar
5 slices bread, cubed
⅓ cup chopped fresh or frozen cranberries
¼ cup white raisins
½ teaspoon salt
3 tablespoons water

1. Trim most of fat from pork chops. Season and brown both sides well in hot bacon fat. Arrange chops in single layer in bottom of slow cooker.
2. Cut four slices from one of the oranges and reserve. Squeeze rest of oranges to make half cup of liquid. Add water if there

is not enough orange juice. Add brown sugar to juice and stir. Pour mixture over the chops.

3. Cover and cook on Low 4 hours.
4. Mix bread cubes, cranberries, raisins, salt, and 3 tablespoons water in a small bowl. Place orange slice on top of each pork chop. Place a small mound of fruit mixture on each slice.
5. Cover slow cooker and cook on Low another 2-4 hours until tender.

Menu

Orangeberry Pork Chops
Green Beans
Potato Pancakes
Applesauce
Chocolate Cupcakes

Pork Chop Bean Bake

Cooking time: 6-8 hours

4 pork chops
3 tablespoons cooking oil
2 cans baked beans
4 peeled apple slices
¼ cup brown sugar
⅛ teaspoon ground cinammon
Dash of ground cloves

1. Brown pork chops well in hot oil. Place beans in bottom of slow cooker. Place pork chops on top of beans.
2. Toss apple slices in mixture of brown sugar, cinammon, and cloves. Place apple slices on top of pork chops.

3. Cover and cook on Low 6-8 hours.

Menu

Pork Chop Bean Bake
Cole Slaw
Sliced Tomatoes
Corn Sticks
Mocha Chip Ice Cream

Baked Ham Slice

Cooking time: 7 hours

1 slice cooked ham cut in four serving pieces
4 cloves
4 tablespoons brown sugar
4 tablespoons fine dry bread crumbs
2 tablespoons white raisins
1 teaspoon dry mustard
1 cup orange juice
1 teaspoon cornstarch
1 tablespoon water

1. Place ham pieces in slow cooker. On each slice place 1 clove, 1 tablespoon brown sugar, 1 tablespoon bread crumbs, several white raisins, ¼ teaspoon dry mustard. (If there is not room in the slow cooker for all four pieces, roll up ham slices with ingredients inside and tie with toothpick or string.)
2. Pour orange juice slowly over top of ham.
3. Cover and cook on High 1 hour; turn to Low and cook another 6 hours.
4. Remove ham from pot. Combine paste of cornstarch and

water and stir into cooking liquid. Turn to High and simmer until thick. Serve over ham.

Menu

Baked Ham Slice
Scalloped Potatoes Parmesan
Fried Eggplant
Mixed Fruit Salad with Sherry Dressing
White Cake with Strawberry Frosting

Ham Jubilee

Cooking time: 7 hours

- 1 slice precooked ham, 1-2 inches thick
- 1 1-pound 4-ounce can pitted black cherries with juice
- ¼ teaspoon each ground cloves, curry powder, cinnamon, dry mustard
- 1 tablespoon white wine vinegar
- 1 cup currant jelly
- ½ cup orange juice
- ¼ cup grated orange rind

1. Bring cherry juice, spices, vinegar, jelly, and orange juice to a boil in saucepan. Reduce heat and let simmer a few seconds. Remove from stove and stir in grated orange rind and cherries.
2. Trim excess fat from ham and slash edges in several places to keep it from curling. Place in slow cooker. Pour sauce over ham.
3. Cook covered on High for 1 hour; turn to Low and cook another 6 hours. Pour sauce over ham slice before serving.

Menu

Ham Jubilee
Lima Beans
Rice and Pineapple Casserole
Gingerbread

Ham and Cheese Casserole

Cooking time: 6-7 hours

- 1 slice cooked ham, diced (enough to make 2 cups)
- 3 tablespoons flour
- ½ teaspoon salt
- 2 teaspoons dry mustard
- 1 teaspoon paprika
- 1 pound Cheddar or Swiss cheese, grated
- 1 tablespoon butter
- 1 12-ounce can of beer
- ½ cup water
- 1 8-ounce package noodles, uncooked

1. Mix flour, salt, dry mustard, and paprika in mixing bowl. Stir in grated cheese. Melt butter in saucepan. Add cheese and flour mixture to butter and stir until cheese is melted and mixture is smooth. Stir in beer and water gradually and continue stirring over low heat until blended.
2. Place diced ham and uncooked noodles in slow cooker. Stir together with cheese sauce.
3. Cover and cook on Low 6-7 hours (High 2-3 hours).

Menu

Ham and Cheese Casserole
Avocado and Grapefruit Salad
Butterscotch-Chip Ice Cream

Black-eyed Peas and Ham Hocks

Cooking time: 10½-11½ hours

1 pound dried black-eyed peas
2 pounds ham hocks
4 cups boiling water
2 medium onions, chopped
1 chopped celery stalk
1 small bay leaf
1 clove garlic
1 small (8-ounce) can tomato purée
2 tablespoons chili sauce

1. Rinse black-eyed peas. Soak in water overnight. (You may also use frozen black-eyed peas. Add them straight from the package to the slow cooker and add only 2 cups of water instead of 4.)
2. Cover ham hocks with boiling water in large pot and boil for 30 minutes.
3. Remove meat with slotted spoon. Drain black-eyed peas and place with meat in slow cooker along with 4 cups of water used to boil ham hocks (2 cups if using frozen peas). Add onions, celery, bay leaf, garlic, tomato purée, and chili sauce.
4. Cover and cook on High 2 hours; then turn to Low and cook another 8-9 hours.

Menu

Black-eyed Peas and Ham Hocks
Mixed Greens
Corn Muffins
Applesauce Cake

4

Poultry and Game

Chicken, the all-American favorite, is a natural for slow cooking. Duck and turkey, too often relegated to the occasional holiday feast, also make satisfying meals any day of the year. If you find you are bored with the familiar taste of fried or broiled chicken, experiment with your slow cooker, using herbs, spices, marinades, and flavorful sauces to impart new glamor and taste to any variety of poultry.

Slow cooking tenderizes poultry, just as it does meat. You can buy less expensive, more mature birds for use in the slow cooker. For most dishes, browning is recommended before cooking; as with meats, browning improves the appearance and flavor. Most poultry dishes will take about 6-8 hours on the Low setting or 4 hours on High. Pan juices make excellent gravy or sauces; for gravy, slowly mix in a paste made of ¼ cup flour and ¼ cup water or milk.

The flavor of wild game is also greatly enhanced by the slow cooking method. Follow a basic cookbook's instructions for cleaning and handling game, use a marinade to take away the "gamey" flavor, and be sure to cook the meat long enough. It is better to cook game the maximum length of time suggested rather than take a chance of undercooking.

Barbecued Chicken

Cooking time: 6-8 hours

1 3½-pound frying chicken cut into serving pieces
¼ cup butter
1 medium chopped onion
2 tablespoons vinegar
2 tablespoons brown sugar
½ clove garlic, minced
¼ cup lemon juice
1 cup catsup
2 teaspoons mustard
½ cup water
3 tablespoons Worcestershire sauce

1. Brown chicken in melted butter over medium heat. Place in slow cooker and pour pan drippings over chicken. Add remaining ingredients.
2. Cover and cook on Low 6-8 hours.

Menu

Barbecued Chicken
Corn Casserole
Apple Salad with Lemon Dressing
Strawberry Shortcake

Lemon and Rosemary Chicken

Cooking time: 6-8 hours

1 3½-pound frying chicken cut into serving pieces
1½ teaspoons salt

- Freshly ground pepper
- 3 tablespoons vegetable oil
- 1 minced clove garlic
- ¼ teaspoon rosemary
- ¼ cup lemon juice
- ⅓ cup butter or margarine, melted
- 2 tablespoons chopped parsley

1. Season chicken and brown well in hot oil in skillet. Place chicken in slow cooker.
2. Combine minced garlic, rosemary, lemon juice, melted butter, and parsley. Pour over chicken.
3. Cover and cook on Low 6-8 hours.

Menu

Lemon and Rosemary Chicken
Potato Puffs Parmesan
Peas and Mushrooms
Hot Rolls
French Tomato Salad
Charlotte Russe

Chicken Louisianne

Cooking time: 6-8 hours

- 1 3-pound broiling chicken cut into serving pieces
- 3 tablespoons olive oil
- 1 chicken bouillon cube
- ¼ cup boiling water
- 1 small chopped onion
- 1 diced green pepper
- ½ clove garlic, minced
- ½ bay leaf

- ½ teaspoon parsley flakes
- ½ teaspoon oregano
- 1 6-ounce can tomato purée
- 2 tablespoons brown sugar
- 2 tablespoons prepared mustard
- 1 teaspoon salt
- ¼ teaspoon pepper
- ¼ cup vinegar
- 1 tablespoon Worcestershire sauce
- ¼ teaspoon cayenne
- 1 6-ounce can mushrooms, drained

1. Heat oil in skillet and brown chicken well on all sides. Place in slow cooker.
2. Dissolve bouillon cube in boiling water. Combine remaining ingredients with bouillon; pour mixture over chicken.
3. Cover and cook on Low 6-8 hours.

Menu

Chicken Louisianne
Wild Rice
Corn Creole
Tossed Salad with French Dressing
Pecan Pie

Chicken Marengo

Cooking time: 8-10 hours

- 3 pounds chicken parts
- 3 tablespoons butter or margarine
- 1 can tomato soup
- 1 can golden mushroom soup
- 1 pound (16) small whole white onions

1 medium clove garlic, minced
¼ teaspoon dried tarragon
Freshly ground pepper

1. Combine soups, onions, garlic, tarragon, and pepper in large bowl. Stir.
2. Brown chicken parts in butter in frying pan. Remove and place in slow cooker. Pour sauce over chicken.
3. Cover and cook on Low 8-10 hours. If sauce is not thick enough after cooking required length of time, uncover, and turn to High, and cook until sauce reaches desired consistency.

Menu

Chicken Marengo
Buttered Egg Noodles
Braised Broccoli
Fudge Layer Cake

Chicken à l'Orange

Cooking time: 6-8 hours

1 3-4-pound frying chicken cut into serving pieces
⅓ cup butter
⅓ cup flour
2 tablespoons brown sugar
1 teaspoon salt
½ teaspoon ginger
½ teaspoon pepper
½ cup orange juice
1 orange, pared and sectioned

1. Melt butter in skillet; brown chicken well on all sides. Remove chicken pieces; place in slow cooker. Blend flour,

brown sugar, salt, ginger, and pepper into pan drippings. Cook until bubbles appear. Stir in orange juice.

2. Place orange sections on top of chicken pieces in slow cooker. Pour orange juice mixture slowly over the top.
3. Cover and cook on Low 6-8 hours.

Menu

Chicken à l'Orange
Long Grain Rice
Asparagus
Almond Cookies

Chicken in Wine Sauce

Cooking time: 6-8 hours

1	3-4-pound chicken cut into serving pieces
¼	pound butter or margarine
1	teaspoon salt
	Freshly ground pepper
	Paprika
	Worcestershire sauce
	Garlic powder
	Parsley flakes
1	cup dry red wine

1. Melt 3 tablespoons of butter or margarine in skillet. Brown chicken well on all sides. Place chicken in slow cooker. Sprinkle with salt, pepper, paprika, Worcestershire sauce, garlic powder, and parsley. Dot with remaining butter. Pour wine over top.
2. Cover and cook on Low 6-8 hours.

Menu

Chicken in Wine Sauce
Peas Braised with Onions and Lettuce
French Bread
Salad of Mixed Greens
Strawberry Tart

Sesame Baked Chicken

Cooking time: 7-9 hours

1 2½-3-pound chicken cut into serving pieces
¼ cup sesame seeds
⅔ cup fine cracker crumbs
¼ cup evaporated milk
½ cup melted butter or margarine
Salt and pepper to taste
½ teaspoon parsley flakes

1. Preheat oven to 350°. Sprinkle sesame seeds on cookie sheet and bake in preheated oven 10 minutes, stirring once or twice. Combine seeds and cracker crumbs.
2. Dip chicken in evaporated milk, roll in crumb mixture, and place in slow cooker. Melt butter or margarine, add parsley, salt, and pepper and pour over top of chicken.
3. Cover and cook on High 1 hour; turn to Low and cook another 6-8 hours.

Menu

Sesame Baked Chicken
Asparagus
Pineapple Rice Casserole
Blueberries and Cream

Chicken Paprika

Cooking time: 6-8 hours

1 3-4-pound chicken cut into serving pieces
1 medium sliced onion
3 tablespoons butter or margarine
1 teaspoon salt
1 teaspoon paprika
½ cup water
1 teaspoon flour
1 pint sour cream

1. Melt butter or margarine in skillet and sauté onion until soft. Remove and add chicken. Brown chicken well on all sides and place in slow cooker.
2. Return onions to pan; add salt, paprika, water, flour, and sour cream. Stir well. Pour over chicken.
3. Cover slow cooker and cook on Low 6-8 hours. (This may be cooked on High 2½-3½ hours, but if you cook on High, do not add sour cream until last 30 minutes of cooking.)

Menu

Chicken Paprika
Hot Buttered Noodles
French-Style Green Beans
Apple Strudel

Chicken Continental

Cooking time: 7-10 hours

1 3-pound chicken cut into serving pieces
2 teaspoons salt

¼ teaspoon pepper
½ teaspoon paprika
3 tablespoons vegetable oil
1 medium chopped onion
¼ cup dry sherry
¼ cup water
1 cup sliced mushrooms
¼ cup mayonnaise
¼ cup sour cream
1 tablespoon snipped parsley
Salt and pepper, to taste

1. Season chicken with salt, pepper, and paprika. Heat vegetable oil in skillet. Brown chicken well on both sides over moderate heat.
2. Remove chicken to slow cooker. Add onion, sherry, and water.
3. Cover and cook on Low 7-10 hours (High 2½-3½ hours, doubling amounts of water and sherry.)
4. When chicken is cooked, remove and keep in warm oven while you make sauce. Stir mushrooms, mayonnaise, and sour cream into pan juices. Add parsley, salt, and pepper to taste. Heat sauce but do not allow it to boil.

Menu

Chicken Continental
Asparagus Spears
Steamed Rice
Peeled Grapes with French Dressing
Profiteroles

Honey-baked Chicken

Cooking time: 6-8 hours

1 3-4-pound chicken cut into serving pieces
3 tablespoons vegetable oil

3 tablespoons butter or margarine
½ cup honey
¼ cup prepared mustard
1 teaspoon salt
1 teaspoon curry powder

1. Brown chicken well in hot oil in skillet. Place in slow cooker.
2. Melt butter or margarine in saucepan. Add remaining ingredients and stir well. Pour over chicken.
3. Cover and cook on Low 6-8 hours.

Menu

Honey-baked Chicken
Potatoes Anna
Brussels Sprouts
Orange and Grapefruit Salad
Green Tomato Pie

Sour Cherry Chicken

Cooking time: 6-8 hours

1 3½-pound frying chicken cut into serving pieces
1 1-pound can pitted red sour cherries packed in water
½ teaspoon salt
Freshly ground pepper
¼ teaspoon paprika
3 tablespoons margarine
1 tablespoon flour
1 teaspoon brown sugar
⅛ teaspoon cinnamon
⅛ teaspoon allspice
1 9-ounce can pineapple chunks
1 chicken bouillon cube
¼ teaspoon red food coloring

1. Drain cherries, saving liquid. Season chicken with salt, pepper, and paprika. Melt butter or margarine in skillet and brown chicken on both sides. Place chicken in slow cooker.
2. To skillet drippings, add flour, sugar, cinnamon, allspice, cherry liquid, pineapple, bouillon cube, and red food coloring. Stir well. Pour over chicken.
3. Cover and cook on Low 6-8 hours. About 20 minutes before serving, add cherries. Serve chicken with sauce poured over it.

Menu

Sour Cherry Chicken
Creamed Potatoes
Peas and Mushrooms
Pear Salad with French Dressing
Marble Cake

Chicken Bombay

Cooking time: 6-8 hours

1 3½-4-pound chicken cut into serving pieces
1 teaspoon salt
Freshly ground pepper
1 teaspoon paprika
3 tablespoons vegetable oil
2 tablespoons brown sugar
½ teaspoon ground ginger
¼ cup rosé wine
2 tablespoons water
¼ cup soy sauce
¼ cup toasted sesame seeds for garnish

1. Season chicken with salt, pepper, and paprika. Brown chicken well in hot oil in skillet.

2. Place chicken in slow cooker. Combine remaining ingredients and pour over chicken. Top with toasted sesame seeds.
3. Cover and cook on Low 6-8 hours.

Menu

Chicken Bombay
Wild Rice
Chinese Pea Pods
Pineapple Salad
Pound Cake

Chicken Calvados

Cooking time: 6-8 hours

1 3½-4-pound chicken cut into serving pieces
4 tablespoons butter
¼ cup warm apple brandy or cognac
¼ cup minced onions
1 teaspoon salt
Freshly ground pepper
⅛ teaspoon sweet basil
2 medium apples, peeled, cored, and diced
½ cup cider
½ cup heavy cream

1. Melt butter in skillet and brown chicken well on all sides. Pour brandy over chicken and set aflame. When flames die down, remove chicken to slow cooker.
2. Combine remaining ingredients except cream, pour over chicken.
3. Cover and cook on Low 6-8 hours. Just before serving, remove chicken; stir in cream until sauce thickens. Serve over chicken.

Menu

Chicken Calvados
Steamed Rice
Baby Peas and Pearl Onions in Artichoke Bottoms
Lime Sherbet

Chicken Seville

Cooking time: 6-8 hours

1 4-5-pound chicken
3 tablespoons olive oil
1 cup chopped onion
½ cup chopped green pepper
2 cloves garlic, minced
1 tablespoon minced parsley
1 8-ounce can tomato sauce
½ cup dry white wine
1 cup boiling water
2 teaspoons salt
¼ teaspoon dried ground red pepper
½ cup seedless raisins
4 cups raw rice
½ cup Cheddar cheese

1. Heat olive oil in skillet and sauté onion and green pepper for about 5 minutes. Add minced garlic, parsley, and chicken and cook over medium heat 15 minutes. Remove ingredients to slow cooker.
2. Add to slow cooker tomato sauce, wine, water, salt, and red pepper.
3. Cover and cook on Low 4-6 hours.
4. Remove chicken and cut meat from bones. Return to slow

cooker with rice and raisins. Stir well. Sprinkle cheese over top, turn to High and cook an additional 2 hours.

If you wish, you may cut chicken into serving pieces. In this case in step 4, remove chicken from slow cooker, stir in rice and raisins, sprinkle cheese on top, and arrange chicken pieces on top of casserole.

Menu

Chicken Seville
Green Fried Bananas
Tossed Salad with Oil and Vinegar Dressing
Fresh Pineapple

Chicken Buffet

Cooking time: 6-8 hours

1	3½-4-pound chicken cut into serving pieces
8	tablespoons butter
12	small peeled white onions
3	medium finely diced potatoes
1	1-inch-thick slice cooked ham, diced
	Freshly ground pepper
½	teaspoon salt
1	minced garlic clove
¼	teaspoon tarragon
4-6	sprigs fresh parsley

1. Melt 4 tablespoons of butter in skillet and brown chicken well on both sides. Meanwhile, melt remaining butter in bottom of slow cooker.
2. Brown onions, potatoes, and ham in skillet. Season with salt

and pepper and add garlic. Remove contents of skillet to slow cooker. Place chicken on top. Sprinkle tarragon over chicken.

3. Cover and cook on Low 6-8 hours. To serve, pour juices from slow cooker over top of casserole and accent with sprigs of parsley.

Menu

Chicken Buffet
Romaine Lettuce Salad with Shrimp Dressing
Spiked Honeydew Melon

Turkey Casserole

Cooking time: 5-8 hours

- 2 cups cooked diced turkey
- 2 cups dry white wine
- ½ cup sliced onion
- ½ bay leaf, crumbled
- 1 teaspoon salt
- ¼ teaspoon pepper
- 1 minced garlic clove
- 1 1-pound can of tomatoes, drained
- ¼ teaspoon cinnamon
- 1 cup uncooked wild rice

1. Combine all ingredients except rice. Place in slow cooker and mix well.
2. Cover and cook on Low 4-6 hours.
3. Stir in rice, turn to High, and cook an additional 1-2 hours or until rice is tender.

Menu

Turkey Casserole
White Wine
Tossed Salad with French Dressing
Mincemeat Pie

Cornish Game Hens

Cooking time: 6-8 hours

- 4 Rock Cornish hens split in half
- 7 tablespoons melted butter
- 2 teaspoons Kitchen Bouquet or other gravy coloring
- 1 small chopped onion
- 1 6-ounce can mushrooms
- 1 5-ounce can sliced water chestnuts
- ½ cup white wine
- 1 chicken bouillon cube
- 3 tablespoons cornstarch
- ¼ cup water

1. Brush hens with 4 tablespoons butter and Kitchen Bouquet. Broil ten minutes on each side.
2. Melt 3 tablespoons butter in skillet and sauté onion until tender. Drain mushrooms and chestnuts, reserving liquid. To this liquid add white wine and enough water to make one pint. Add to skillet and bring to boil. Stir in bouillon cube. Mix cornstarch with water and add to skillet. Cook until sauce is transparent.
3. Place hens in slow cooker and pour sauce over top. Add chestnuts and mushrooms.
4. Cover and cook on Low 6-8 hours.

Menu

Cornish Game Hens
Steamed Rice
Bibb Lettuce with Orange Dressing
French Pastry

Peruvian Duck

Cooking time: 8-10 hours

1 4-5-pound duck, with fat trimmed, cut into 6-8 pieces
¼ cup lemon juice
½ teaspoon ground cumin seeds
1 teaspoon salt
Freshly ground pepper
¼ cup olive oil
4 cups light beer
2 cups uncooked long grain rice
1 cup finely chopped fresh coriander
1 cup cooked fresh or frozen peas

1. In mixing bowl, combine lemon juice, cumin seeds, and ½ teaspoon each of salt and pepper. Coat duck with mixture. Cover bowl in foil and marinate at room temperature approximately 3 hours or in refrigerator about 6 hours.
2. In skillet, heat olive oil until light haze forms. Brown duck well in hot oil.
3. Remove 1 tablespoon of fat from skillet and put into slow cooker with duck and 1 cup beer.
4. Cover and cook on Low 8-10 hours.
5. About 30 minutes before serving, remove ½ cup of liquid from slow cooker. Combine with 3 cups beer in a saucepan.

Bring to a boil, add rice, ½ teaspoon salt, and freshly ground pepper. Reduce heat, cover, and simmer 20 minutes or until liquid is absorbed.

5. Stir in coriander and peas. Serve immediately with duck. (Fresh coriander can be found in Oriental and Latin American supermarkets.)

Menu

Peruvian Duck
Coriander Rice with Peas
Tossed Salad
Bananas Flambé

Duck Bayou

Cooking time: 8-10 hours

- 1 4-5-pound duckling
- 2 teaspoons salt
- ¼ teaspoon pepper
- ¼ cup presifted flour
- ¼ cup butter or margarine
- 1 medium sliced onion
- ½ minced garlic clove
- 1 cup red wine
- ½ cup diced cooked ham
- ½ bay leaf
- ½ teaspoon parsley flakes
- ¼ teaspoon tarragon
- 1 8-ounce can mushrooms, drained
- 2 tablespoons cornstarch

1. Combine salt, pepper, and flour in a bag. Add pieces of duck and shake to coat.

2. Melt butter or margarine in skillet and brown duck well on all sides. Place in slow cooker.
3. In skillet, sauté onion and garlic in remaining butter. Add wine, ham, ½ bay leaf, parsley flakes, and tarragon. Bring to a boil. Pour over top of duck in slow cooker.
4. Cover and cook on Low 8-10 hours. Add mushrooms during last half hour. When duck is cooked, remove it from the slow cooker. Add cornstarch to liquid in pot and stir until thickened. Pour over duck and serve.

Menu

Duck Bayou
Wild and Long Grain Rice
Tomato Pudding
Chess Pie

Wild Duck in Orange Sauce

Cooking time: 8-10 hours

1	wild duck cut into serving pieces
	Salt and freshly ground pepper
¼	cup bacon drippings
1	cup beef broth
1	cup orange juice
3	tablespoons grated orange rind
½	cup dry vermouth
⅓	cup light brown sugar
	Flour

1. Season duck and brown well in bacon drippings in skillet. Remove to slow cooker. Add remaining ingredients.
2. Cover and cook on Low 8-10 hours. Thicken pan juices with flour if necessary.

Menu

Wild Duck in Orange Sauce
Brown Rice with Chestnuts
Currant Jelly
Watercress Salad with Orange Dressing
Pumpkin Cake

Game Birds in Wine

Cooking time: 6-8 hours

- 2 pheasants, partridges, or grouse
- 1 medium sliced onion
- 2 bay leaves
- 1 minced garlic clove
- 4 cups white wine
- 1½ teaspoons salt
- ½ teaspoon pepper
- ¼ cup flour seasoned with salt and pepper to taste
- 4 tablespoons butter
- 1 tablespoon flour

1. Combine sliced onion, bay leaves, garlic, white wine, salt, and pepper in large bowl or glass baking dish. Add game birds and marinate in refrigerator for 2-3 days.
2. Coat birds with seasoned flour. Melt 3 tablespoons butter and brown game birds well on all sides. Transfer to slow cooker and add strained marinade.
3. Cover and cook on Low 6-8 hours. Thicken sauce with mixture of 1 tablespoon butter and 1 tablespoon flour. Pour over each serving. Serves 4-6.

Menu

Game Birds in Wine
Wild Rice
Chicory Salad
Gooseberry Conserve
Pineapple Sherbet

Pheasant on Toast

Cooking time: 6-8 hours

2 pheasants cut in serving pieces
¼ cup flour
2 teaspoons salt
Freshly ground pepper
3 tablespoons butter
2 medium onions, chopped
½ cup sweet vermouth
1 teaspoon tomato paste
⅛ teaspoon cinnamon
6 slices toast
Watercress

1. Coat pheasants with mixture of flour, 1 teaspoon salt, and pepper. Melt butter in skillet and brown pheasant pieces. Place pheasant in slow cooker.
2. In skillet, sauté onions until transparent. Transfer to slow cooker. Add vermouth, tomato paste, cinnamon, 1 teaspoon salt, and pepper. Stir well.
3. Cover and cook on Low 6-8 hours. Place pheasant on toast; top with sauce and garnish with watercress. Serves 6.

Menu

Pheasant on Toast
Braised Cabbage
Purée of Chestnuts
Raspberry Sundae

Venison Stew

Cooking time: 7-12 hours

2-3 pounds venison stew meat cut in one-inch cubes
½ cup bacon fat

1 can cream of celery soup
2 soup cans of water
Juice of ½ lemon
Dash of Worcestershire sauce
1 minced garlic clove
2-3 bay leaves
Salt and pepper to taste
Dash of paprika
Pinch of allspice
1 cup sliced carrots
6-8 small whole white onions
4 cups cubed potatoes
1 cup cut-up turnip
1 package frozen peas

1. Brown meat in skillet in hot bacon fat. Place in slow cooker with remaining ingredients.
2. Cover and cook on Low 7-12 hours. Serve over rice or buttered noodles. Serves 6-8.

Menu

Venison Stew
Rice or Buttered Noodles
Salad of Mixed Greens
Bran Muffins
Poached Pears

Venison Steak

Cooking time: 8-10 hours

2-3 pounds venison steak
1½ cups Burgundy wine
2 large sliced onions

- 1 whole clove
- 1/8 teaspoon thyme
- Dash of nutmeg
- Dash of cayenne
- 1/2 garlic clove
- 1/4 cup flour
- 1/2 teaspoon salt
- Freshly ground pepper
- 3 tablespoons butter
- 2 cups canned tomatoes
- 1 1/2 tablespoons Worcestershirs sauce
- 1 small can sliced mushrooms

1. Combine wine, onions, clove, thyme, nutmeg, cayenne, and garlic in large bowl. Marinate venison in this mixture in refrigerator overnight.
2. Remove venison, reserving marinade. Coat steak lightly in seasoned flour. Melt butter in skillet and brown steak on both sides.
3. Place venison in slow cooker. Add strained marinade, tomatoes and Worcestershire sauce.
4. Cover and cook 8-10 hours on Low. Add mushrooms during last half hour.

Menu

Venison Steak
Brussels Sprouts and Chestnuts
Salad of Mixed Greens
Rolls with Currant Jelly
Fresh Fruit

5

Seafood

Although most fish tastes best when cooked quickly at a high heat, there are some shellfish recipes that adapt well to the slow cooker. Shellfish should never be cooked longer than 6 hours, however, and often may be added only an hour or two before serving.

Shellfish simmered in a highly seasoned sauce is delicious when prepared in the slow cooker. Most of the recipes in this chapter can be cooked unattended during an afternoon, and many are suitable for buffet serving. Dishes such as shrimp or lobster curry and shrimp creole can be kept warm in the slow cooker for several hours during a cocktail party or buffet dinner.

Clam Sauce for Pasta

Cooking time: 12-18 hours

2 cups chopped clams, fresh or canned
3 tablespoons olive oil
1 small chopped onion
1 finely chopped garlic clove
1 large can (1-pound 12-ounces) Italian Plum tomatoes, drained
1 can tomato paste
⅓ cup finely chopped parsley
1 teaspoon oregano
1 teaspoon salt
1 tomato paste can of water (optional)
1 cup sliced mushrooms (optional)
1 pound pasta
Parmesan or Romano cheese

(This Italian delicacy also can be made with crab meat.)

1. Heat oil in skillet and sauté onion and garlic until onion is golden. Place in slow cooker. Add tomatoes, tomato paste, parsley, oregano, and salt.
2. Cover and cook on Low 12-18 hours (5-6 hours on High). If sauce appears too thick after cooking half the allotted time, add tomato paste can of water. Add clams and mushrooms the last hour.
3. Serve over spaghetti or other pasta with grated Parmesan or Romano cheese. Serves 6.

Menu

Clam Sauce for Pasta
Salad of Romaine Lettuce
Garlic Bread
Fresh Fruit

Lobster Curry

Cooking time: 5-6 hours

1 pound lobster meat, fresh or canned
3 tablespoons butter
2 medium chopped onions
1 chopped clove garlic
1-2 teaspoons curry powder
Dash of cayenne
Juice of one lemon
1 tablespoon grated lemon peel
1 cup evaporated milk
Salt

1. Melt butter in skillet and sauté onion and garlic until onion is golden. Stir in curry powder and cayenne. Add lemon juice and peel. Slowly stir in evaporated milk. Add lobster. Salt to taste. Transfer to slow cooker.
2. Cover and cook on Low 5-6 hours. Serve over rice.

Menu

Lobster Curry
Rice
Chopped Almonds, Boiled Eggs, Chutney
Spinach Salad
Almond Cookies

Oysters in Mushroom Sauce

Cooking time: 2-4 hours

1 pint oysters and liquid
2 tablespoons butter
2 tablespoons flour

- 1½ cups milk
- ½ cup cream
- ⅛ teaspoon cayenne
- ½ teaspoon salt
- ¼ teaspoon pepper
- ½ pound fresh, sliced mushrooms
- ½ teaspoon Worcestershire sauce

1. Melt butter in a saucepan or skillet; gradually stir in flour over medium heat. Add milk, cream, and oyster liquid slowly, stirring constantly until mixture is smooth. Add cayenne, salt, and pepper. Transfer to slow cooker. Add oysters and mushrooms.
2. Cover and cook on Low 2-4 hours. Stir in Worcestershire sauce and serve.

Menu

Oysters in Mushroom Sauce
Rice
Salad of Belgian Endive
Peas and Pearl Onions
Spice Cake

Shrimp Creole

Cooking time: 3-5 hours

- 3 cups cooked shrimp, peeled and deveined
- 3 tablespoons olive oil
- 1 minced garlic clove
- 1 medium chopped onion
- 1½ cups chopped celery
- 1 coarsely chopped green pepper
- 2 1-pound cans Italian plum tomatoes, drained

3 heaping tablespoons tomato paste
1 teaspoon sugar
1 teaspoon thyme
½ teaspoon Tabasco
Salt and pepper to taste

1. Heat olive oil in skillet and sauté garlic, onion, celery, and green pepper several minutes. Transfer to slow cooker. Add tomatoes, tomato paste, sugar, thyme, salt and pepper, and Tabasco.
2. Cover and cook on Low 3-5 hours. Turn slow cooker to High 35-45 minutes before serving and add shrimp. Serve over rice.

Menu

Shrimp Creole
Rice Jambalaya
Salad of Mixed Greens
Pecan Puffs

Shrimp Curry in Rice Ring

Cooking time: 5-6 hours

2 pounds raw shrimp, peeled and deveined
4 tablespoons butter
1 medium chopped onion
1 large coarsely chopped apple
¼ cup shredded coconut
1 tablespoon curry powder
1½ tablespoons flour
½ teaspoon powdered ginger

½ teaspoon dry mustard
Dash of cayenne
1 cup chicken broth
1 cup cream
Cooked rice

1. Melt butter in skillet and sauté onion and apple. Transfer to slow cooker. Stir in coconut, curry powder, flour, ginger, mustard, and cayenne. Gradually add in chicken broth. Stir until smooth. Slowly add cream, stirring constantly.
2. Cover and cook on Low 4-5 hours. Add shrimp, cover, and cook another hour. Serve over rice.

Menu

Shrimp Curry in Rice Ring
Chopped Peanuts, Chutney, Cherry Tomatoes, Grated Coconut
Salad of Mixed Greens
Peach Pie

Shrimp Regal

Cooking time: 4-6 hours

1 pound cooked shrimp
2 tablespoons butter
¾ pound halved fresh mushrooms
2 tablespoons flour
1 cup milk
¼ cup dry sherry
Salt and pepper to taste
1 tablespoon Worcestershire sauce
1 package frozen artichoke hearts
¼ cup grated Parmesan cheese
Paprika
Chopped parsley

1. Melt butter in skillet and sauté mushrooms lightly. Stir in flour and cook for several minutes, stirring constantly. Gradually pour in milk, and continue stirring until sauce thickens. Stir in sherry, salt, pepper, and Worcestershire sauce.
2. Place artichoke hearts in slow cooker. Add shrimp, and pour sauce from skillet over top. Sprinkle with Parmesan cheese and dust with paprika.
3. Cover and cook on Low 4-6 hours. To serve, sprinkle with chopped parsley.

Menu

Shrimp Regal
Rice
Salad of Mixed Greens
Poached Pears

Baked Salmon

Cooking time: 5-6 hours

1 16-ounce can of red salmon, drained
2 slightly beaten eggs
1½ cups fresh bread crumbs
2 teaspoons grated onion
¼ teaspoon salt
1 tablespoon snipped parsley
1 tablespoon lemon juice
1 cup grated Parmesan cheese
½ cup sliced mushrooms

1. Lightly grease slow cooker. Flake salmon and place in slow cooker with remaining ingredients and stir well.
2. Cover and cook on High 2 hours; then turn to Low and cook another 3-4 hours.

Menu

Baked Salmon
Asparagus
Tossed Salad
Strawberry Tart

Salmon Loaf

Cooking time: 3-5 hours

2 cups canned salmon
3 tablespoons butter
3 tablespoons flour
1 cup milk and salmon liquid combined
Salt and pepper
1 teaspoon dillweed
1 tablespoon minced parsley
1 cup bread crumbs
1 beaten egg

1. Drain canned salmon, reserving the liquid. Melt butter in skillet and slowly stir in flour. Add milk and salmon liquid, gradually stirring. Cook until sauce starts to thicken, stirring constantly.
2. Pour sauce into large mixing bowl. Add salt, pepper, dill, and parsley. Stir in salmon, bread crumbs, and beaten egg. Form the mixture into a loaf. Place in bottom of slow cooker.
3. Cover and cook on High 1 hour; turn to Low and cook an additional 2-4 hours.

Menu

Salmon Loaf
Rice
Cucumber Salad
Lemon Chiffon Pie

Tuna-stuffed Peppers

Cooking time: 3-4 hours

- 4 green peppers
- 1 6-7 ounce can tuna, drained
- 1½ cups dry bread crumbs
- 1 15-ounce can tomato sauce
- 1 teaspoon salt
- ⅛ teaspoon pepper
- 1 teaspoon minced onion
- 2 tablespoons butter or margarine
- 2 slices Swiss cheese, cut in squares

1. Cut tops from green peppers and remove seeds and membranes. Mix together tuna, 1 cup crumbs, 1 cup tomato sauce, salt, pepper, and onion. Fill peppers with tuna mixture and top with rest of bread crumbs. Dot with butter. Place cheese square over top.
2. Pour remainder of tomato sauce into slow cooker. Place stuffed peppers in slow cooker, cover and cook on High 3-4 hours.

Menu

Tuna-stuffed Peppers
Cold Rice Salad
Iced Tea
Green Grapes

6

International Pot Luck

Many popular international dishes were originally cooked slowly over open hearths and so are well suited to the electric slow cooker. This chapter contains recipes from around the world for all types of main course dishes: stews, meat, poultry and game, even a vegetable casserole and a fondue.

Since many of these recipes require a few more steps in preparation than those in other chapters, they may be most conveniently cooked on weekends, when you have more time and meals can be enjoyed in a more leisurely fashion. Most of the dishes are ideal party meals, and the menus that accompany them suggest companion foods that fit the international theme.

Boeuf Bourguignonne

Cooking time: 8-10 hours

- 3 pounds beef chuck cut into 1½-inch cubes
- 1½ cups red wine
- 1 bay leaf
- 1 onion stuck with 2 cloves
- 1 clove garlic
- 6 strips thick bacon cut into half-inch pieces
- 3 tablespoons flour
- 1 teaspoon marjoram
- ½ teaspoon rosemary
- 1 sprig parsley
- 1½ cups bouillon
- Salt and pepper to taste
- 12-18 small white onions
- 3 tablespoons butter
- 1 pound sliced mushrooms

1. Combine red wine, bay leaf, onion, and garlic in glass baking dish. Place beef cubes in mixture and marinate for several hours at room temperature.
2. In skillet, brown bacon until crisp. Remove and drain. Add beef cubes and brown well. Transfer to slow cooker and add bacon and all remaining ingredients except butter and mushrooms.
3. Cover and cook on Low 8-10 hours. Sauté mushrooms in butter and add to slow cooker about one hour before serving.

Menu

Boeuf Bourguignonne
Boiled Potatoes
Salad of Mixed Greens
French Bread
Fresh Fruit

Hungarian Goulash (Gulyas)

Cooking time: 7-10 hours

2 pounds beef chuck cut in one-inch cubes
4 tablespoons butter
3 medium chopped onions
1 tablespoon Hungarian sweet paprika
2 tablespoons flour
2 teaspoons salt
½ teaspoon pepper
Dash of thyme
1 minced garlic clove
1 16-ounce can of tomatoes
1 cup sour cream

1. Melt butter in skillet and sauté onions. Add beef cubes and brown well. Transfer beef cubes and onions to slow cooker.
2. Add remaining ingredients except sour cream. Stir, cover, and cook on Low 7-10 hours, adding sour cream last half hour. Serve over hot buttered noodles.

Menu

Hungarian Goulash
Buttered Noodles
Beet and Lettuce Salad
Apple Strudel

Sauerbraten

Cooking time: 10-12 hours

1 4-5 pound pot roast of beef
¼ cup flour

3 tablespoons vegetable oil
2 sliced carrots
2 quartered onions
1 tablespoon tomato catsup

Marinade

4 cups red wine
1 cup water
Juice of 1 lemon
1 large thinly sliced onion
4-5 peppercorns
2 bay leaves
1 whole clove
Pinch of nutmeg
1 teaspoon parsley flakes

Sauce

2 cups liquid from slow cooker
⅔ cup crushed gingersnaps
2 tablespoons sugar
½ cup red wine
1 cup raisins

1. Combine all marinade ingredients except parsley in large kettle and bring to boil. Remove from heat.
2. Wipe beef and place in a large bowl. Pour marinade over beef and add parsley. Cover and let marinate in refrigerator 2-3 days.
3. Remove beef from marinade. Strain marinade and save. Dredge the beef in flour and sauté in oil until well browned.
4. Place carrots and onions in slow cooker. Add roast, catsup, and one cup of reserved marinade. Cover and cook on Low 10-12 hours.
5. When pot roast is almost done, pour off two cups of cooking liquid. Place in blender with crushed gingersnaps, sugar, wine, and raisins. Blend until fairly smooth. Place in saucepan and cook until thick. Serve with pot roast.

Menu

Sauerbraten
Potato Pancakes with Applesauce
Brussels Sprouts
Salad of Mixed Greens
Raspberry Tart

Persian Casserole

Cooking time: 8-10 hours

1 pound round steak cut into half-inch cubes
4 medium diced apples
1 medium sliced onion
3 tablespoons vegetable oil
¼ teaspoon turmeric
½ cup dry split peas, presoaked
½ teaspoon salt
¾ cup water
Juice of one lemon
1 tablespoon brown sugar

1. Brown apple cubes and onion slices in hot oil until golden. Add turmeric and stir. Remove with slotted spoon and place in slow cooker.
2. Brown meat well on all sides in skillet. Place meat cubes in slow cooker.
3. Add split peas and stir together with meat and apple-onion mixture. Pour salted water over all. Add lemon juice and brown sugar.
4. Cover and cook on Low 8-10 hours.

Menu

Persian Casserole
Saffron Rice
Tossed Salad
Coconut Pie

Flemish Carbonnade of Beef

Cooking time: 8-10 hours

- 3-4 pound beef chuck roast cut in 1-inch cubes
- ½ cup flour
- Freshly ground pepper
- 3 tablespoons butter
- 1 minced clove garlic
- 8-10 whole small white onions
- ½ teaspoon sugar
- 1 12-ounce can beer
- ½ teaspoon vinegar

1. Season meat cubes and coat with flour. Melt butter in skillet. Sauté garlic; add meat and brown well. Place in slow cooker with rest of ingredients.
2. Cover and cook on Low 8-10 hours.

Menu

Flemish Carbonnade of Beef
Asparagus Spears
New Potatoes with Parsley Butter
Stuffed Mushrooms
Coffee Ice Cream

Russian Beef Borscht

Cooking time: 10-12 hours

- 1 pound stew meat cut into half-inch cubes (can be left over pot roast)

1 medium diced onion
1 sliced carrot
1 16-ounce can tomatoes, drained, reserving juice
1 cup diced beets (about 2 medium beets)
1 small head cabbage (½ pound shredded)
½ cup diced raw potatoes
1 teaspoon salt
Freshly ground pepper
½ bay leaf
½ clove garlic, minced
1 teaspoon lemon juice (optional)
Sour cream

1. In slow cooker, combine meat, onion, carrot, tomatoes, beets, cabbage, and potatoes. Add enough water to juice from tomatoes to make one cup liquid. Add to pot. Stir in salt, pepper, bay, and garlic.
2. Cover and cook on Low 10-12 hours. Stir in lemon juice, if desired. Top each serving with sour cream, or stir sour cream into soup for creamy texture.

Menu

Russian Beef Borscht
Dark Rye Bread
Fresh Fruits and Cheese

Italian Meatballs

Cooking time: 4-6 hours

1 pound ground chuck
1 pound Italian sausage
3 tablespoons butter or margarine
1 medium chopped onion
1 8-ounce can tomato sauce
1 6-ounce can tomato paste

1 1-pound 13-ounce can tomato wedges, drained
1½ cups water
1½ teaspoons oregano
1½ teaspoons salt
1 tablespoon sugar
2 teaspoons chopped parsley
½ cup bread crumbs (1 slice bread)
½ cup milk
1 egg
½ clove garlic, minced
3 tablespoons grated Parmesan cheese

1. Melt butter in skillet and sauté half of chopped onion until golden. Put into slow cooker using slotted spoon. Add tomato sauce, tomato paste, can of drained tomatoes, and water to slow cooker. Add 1 teaspoon oregano, ½ teaspoon salt, sugar, and 1 teaspoon chopped parsley. Turn slow cooker to High and simmer sauce while you make meatballs.
2. In large mixing bowl combine bread crumbs, milk, ground meat, sausage, egg, 1 teaspoon salt, ½ teaspoon oregano, minced garlic, grated cheese, 1 teaspoon parsley and remaining onion. Mix well and shape into balls. Brown meatballs in skillet in remaining butter. Add to sauce.
3. Cover, and cook on Low 4-6 hours.

Menu

Italian Meatballs
Mostaccioli
Salad of Romaine Lettuce
Garlic Bread
Spumoni

Côtes de Veau

Cooking time: 7-9 hours

4 veal cutlets
1 medium chopped onion

- 3 tablespoons butter or margarine
- ¼ cup dry white wine
- ¼ cup chicken broth
- ½ teaspoon salt
- ⅛ teaspoon freshly ground black pepper
- 1 slightly beaten egg
- ¼ cup Parmesan or Gruyère cheese, grated
- 2 cups cornflake crumbs

1. Sauté onion in butter until soft and golden in color. Stir in wine and chicken broth and simmer while you prepare the cutlets.
2. Season cutlets and dip in slightly beaten egg. Roll chops in grated cheese, then in crumbs.
3. Put remaining crumbs in bottom of slow cooker. Place cutlets on top of crumbs. Pour wine and chicken broth mixture over cutlets.
4. Cover and cook on High 1 hour; then turn to Low and cook another 6-8 hours.

Menu

Vichyssoise
Côtes de Veau
Glazed Carrots
Salad of Mixed Greens
French Pastries

Swedish Kalvrullader

Cooking time: 7-9 hours

- 2-2½ pounds veal cutlets, about half-inch thick
- ¼ pound boneless pork
- 1½ teaspoon salt
- ¼ teaspoon white pepper
- 2 sliced apples
- 2 tablespoons butter or margarine

1 bouillon cube
1 cup hot water

1. Pound veal cutlets flat and cut each into 2 pieces. Cut slits across the top of the cutlets, about 1½ inches apart, partially through the meat. Cut pork into thin strips and fit into slits in the veal. Season veal with ½ teaspoon salt and ⅛ teaspoon white pepper.
2. Place apple slices on veal. Roll each piece of veal and tie with a string. In a skillet, brown rolls in melted butter until well browned.
3. Dissolve bouillon cube in hot water. Add 1 teaspoon salt and ⅛ teaspoon pepper. Place veal in slow cooker and pour bouillon over the top.
4. Cover and cook on High one hour. Turn to Low for an additional 6-8 hours. Thicken pan juices for gravy if desired. To serve, cut rolls into slices.

Menu

Swedish Kalvrullader
Cucumber Salad
Browned Potatoes
Fresh Fruit with Cheese

Swiss Bernerplatte

Cooking time: 10-12 hours

1 16-ounce can sauerkraut
1 large Idaho potato, peeled and sliced
2-3 pork chops
2 knockwurst sausages
2 Polish sausages (Kielbasa)
Salt and pepper
1 12-ounce can beer

1. Salt and pepper potatoes and chops. Place the following layers in slow cooker: sauerkraut, potatoes, sauerkraut, pork chops, sauerkraut, knockwurst, sauerkraut, Kielbasa. Pour 1 can beer over ingredients.
2. Cover and cook on Low 10-12 hours.

Menu

Swiss Bernerplatte
Black Bread
Beer

Kashmir Lamb Curry

Cooking time: 10-12 hours

2-3 pounds boneless lamb cut in one-inch cubes
1 small grated onion
1 grated clove garlic
1 teaspoon crushed coriander seeds
1 teaspoon salt
1 teaspoon cumin seed
½ teaspoon black pepper
1 teaspoon powdered ginger
1 teaspoon each ground cloves and ground cardamom
½ teaspoon ground cinnamon
¼ cup lemon juice
1 cup yogurt
¼ cup butter
1-2 teaspoons curry powder

1. Mix onion, garlic, coriander, salt, cumin, pepper, ginger, cloves, cardamom, cinnamon, and lemon juice. Beat by hand or in blender until smooth. Add yogurt and butter and blend again.

2. Place lamb cubes in glass baking dish; pour sauce over meat, cover, and let stand 1-2 hours at room temperature or overnight in refrigerator.
3. Place lamb with marinade sauce in slow cooker. Add curry powder to taste. Cover and cook on Low 10-12 hours.

Menu

Kashmir Lamb Curry
Long Grain Rice with Peanuts and Raisins
Mandarin Orange Salad
Darjeeling Tea

Irish Stew

Cooking time: 11-13 hours

- 1½ pounds shoulder of lamb cut in 1-inch cubes
- 6 small thinly sliced white potatoes
- 6 small white onions
- 2½ teaspoons salt
- ½ teaspoon white pepper
- ¼ teaspoon thyme
- 1 bay leaf
- 2 cups water

1. In slow cooker arrange successive layers of potatoes, meat, and onions. Sprinkle each layer with salt, pepper and thyme. Add bay leaf and water.
2. Cover and cook on High 1 hour; turn to Low and cook additional 10-12 hours.

Menu

Irish Stew
Bran Muffins
Tossed Salad with Grated Carrots
Butter Pecan Ice Cream

Aloha Spareribs

Cooking time: 6-8 hours

- 4 pounds spareribs
- 1 teaspoon salt
- ¼ cup soy sauce
- ½ cup cooking oil
- ¾ cup pineapple juice
- 2 tablespoons brown sugar
- ¼ cup cider vinegar
- 1 cup plus 1 tablespoon water
- 1 teaspoon cornstarch
- 1 cup pineapple chunks

1. Cut spareribs into individual ribs, removing excess fat. Combine ½ teaspoon salt and soy sauce and brush on ribs. Heat cooking oil in skillet. Brown ribs and place in slow cooker.
2. To skillet juices add pineapple juice, remaining salt, sugar, vinegar, water, and cornstarch. Stir over medium temperature until smooth. Add pineapple chunks. Pour over spareribs.
3. Cover and cook on Low for 6-8 hours.

Menu

Aloha Spareribs
Green Rice
Mandarin Orange Salad
Coconut Cream Pie

Parisian Oxtail Stew

Cooking time: 10-12 hours

- 4 pounds oxtails cut in two-inch pieces
- 1 chopped carrot

- 2 chopped onions
- 8 whole black peppercorns
- 1 teaspoon salt
- ⅛ teaspoon poultry seasoning
- 2 cups Burgundy wine
- 1 bouquet garni (3-inch long piece of celery, 4 sprigs parsley, pinch of dried thyme, 1 bay leaf tied in cheesecloth bag)
- 3 tablespoons shortening
- 3 tablespoons butter
- 12 small white onions
- 3 sliced carrots
- ½ teaspoon sugar
- 3 tablespoons flour
- 1 minced garlic clove
- 1 cup canned tomato purée
- ½ pound sliced mushrooms
- 1 tablespoon salt
- 2 cups water

1. In bowl, combine chopped carrot and onions, peppercorns, 1 teaspoon salt, poultry seasoning, wine, and bouquet garni. Add oxtails and marinate in refrigerator for 3 hours or overnight.
2. Remove oxtails from marinade. Brown them in melted shortening in skillet. Place in slow cooker. Wipe skillet clean, melt butter, and sauté whole onions and sliced carrots until lightly browned. Sprinkle with ½ teaspoon sugar. Place in slow cooker along with flour, garlic, tomato purée, mushrooms, 1 tablespoon salt, and 2 cups water. Add marinade with bouquet garni and vegetables. Stir ingredients together.
3. Cover and cook on Low 10-12 hours. Skim off fat occasionally. Serves 6-8.

Menu

Parisian Oxtail Stew
Crusty French Bread
Strawberry Tart

Bavarian Dinner

Cooking time: 5-7 hours

1½ pounds knockwurst
2 pounds sauerkraut
3 cups grated boiling potatoes
2 cups sour cream
¼ teaspoon pepper
½ teaspoon caraway seeds

1. Cook knockwurst in boiling water. Drain and keep over low heat until skin browns slightly. Cut in 2-inch pieces.
2. Rinse and drain sauerkraut and mix with knockwurst, potatoes, sour cream, pepper, and caraway seeds in slow cooker.
3. Cover and cook on Low 5-7 hours.

Menu

Bavarian Dinner
Green Beans
Cucumber Salad
Lemon Cake

Chicken Teriyaki

Cooking time: 6-8 hours

6 chicken breasts
½ cup soy sauce
½ cup white wine or orange juice
1 medium chopped onion
½ cup sugar (use brown sugar if orange juice is used)
¼ teaspoon ginger

¼ teaspoon cloves
1 minced clove garlic

1. Combine soy sauce, wine or orange juice, onion, sugar, ginger, cloves, and garlic. Pour over chicken and marinate for two hours. (If desired, chicken can be deboned and cut into cubes.) Remove chicken with marinade to slow cooker.
2. Cover and cook on Low for 6-8 hours. Serve with sauce over rice.

Menu

Chicken Teriyaki
Rice
Curried Fruit
Peanut Butter Cookies

Paella

Cooking time: 9-13 hours

1½-2 pounds cut up chicken
1 thinly sliced carrot
2 small diced onions
2 celery stalks with leaves
4 cups water
½ teaspoon oregano
½ teaspoon paprika
¼ teaspoon freshly ground pepper
2½ teaspoons salt
¼ cup olive oil
1 cup long grain rice
1 garlic clove
½ teaspoon ground saffron

1 medium-sized sweet red pepper, seeded, deribbed and cut into one-and-one-half-inch strips
¾ pound uncooked frozen shrimp (not thawed)
12 small clams in shell (or one 8-10-ounce can)
½ cup frozen peas

(Feel free to vary the ingredients in this famous Spanish dish; there are hundreds of versions, the only common ingredients being olive oil, saffron, and rice. Other additions or substitutions include lobster, mussels, chorizo sausage, rabbit, artichokes or string beans instead of peas, green instead of red pepper.)

1. Place carrot, onions, and celery in slow cooker. Place chicken pieces on top. Pour in 4 cups water. Sprinkle oregano, paprika, pepper, and ½ teaspoon of the salt over all.
2. Cover and cook on Low 7-10 hours (or on High 2½-3½ hours).
3. Remove chicken; strain and reserve liquid. Discard vegetables. Bone chicken and cut meat into pieces. Return chicken to cooker.
4. Heat olive oil in skillet. Cook rice and garlic until well browned. Add these to slow cooker. Add saffron and 2 teaspoons salt and stir. Add red pepper, shrimp, and clams and stir. (If fresh clams are used, add them last, placing them on top of other ingredients.) Pour in 2 cups strained stock from chicken.
5. Cover and cook on High 2-3 hours. Add peas during last hour of cooking.

(If you wish, you may pan- or oven-fry chicken separately and serve it over the paella. In this case, add two cups of canned chicken stock to slow cooker as liquid.)

Menu

Paella
Green Fried Bananas
Salad of Mixed Greens
Flan

Coq au Vin

Cooking time: 6-8 hours

- 1 4½-pound roasting chicken cut in serving pieces
- 4 diced slices bacon
- 8-10 pearl onions
- ½ pound fresh whole mushrooms
- Salt
- Pepper
- Flour
- 3 tablespoons butter
- 3 tablespoons oil
- 2 crushed garlic cloves
- 1 tablespoon dried parsley flakes
- 2 bay leaves
- ½ teaspoon thyme
- 2 cups dry white wine

1. Fry bacon slowly until crisp. Remove and place on paper towel to drain excess fat. Brown onions in skillet until tender. Remove onions and sauté mushrooms lightly.
2. Add salt and pepper to flour in a bag; shake chicken to lightly coat each piece. Pour fat from skillet. Add butter and oil, heat, and brown chicken well.
3. Place chicken in slow cooker. Sprinkle crushed garlic, parsley flakes, bay leaves, and thyme over chicken. Add bacon bits, onions, and mushrooms. Pour wine over top.

4. Cover and cook on Low 6-8 hours.
5. Mix flour and water with pan juices to make gravy. Serve over chicken.

Menu

Coq au Vin
Buttered New Potatoes
Artichoke Salad
Pears and Cheese

Chicken Hacienda

Cooking time: 6-8 hours

1	3-4 pound chicken cut up
¼	cup vegetable oil
1-1½	tablespoons chili powder
¼	teaspoon pepper
¼	teaspoon cinnamon
1½	teaspoons grated onion
1	teaspoon salt
1	20-ounce can pineapple chunks
2	ripe bananas
1	ripe avocado or melon
½	pound seedless white grapes

1. Brown chicken well on all sides in hot oil in skillet. Place chicken in slow cooker. Sprinkle chili powder, pepper, cinnamon, onion, and salt over chicken. Pour pineapple chunks with juice over all.
2. Cover slow cooker and cook on Low 6-8 hours.
3. Remove chicken from slow cooker and place on serving platter. Peel and quarter bananas and avocado. Arrange bananas, avocado, and grapes around or over chicken. Pour cooking liquid over all.

Menu

Chicken Hacienda
Rice and Raisin Casserole
Flan

Hasenpfeffer

Cooking time: 8-10 hours

2	2-pound hares or rabbits dressed and cut up
1½	cups dry red wine
½	cup cider vinegar
1	bay leaf
1	medium sliced onion
6	tablespoons flour
2	teaspoons salt
3	tablespoons butter
2	small chopped onions
¼	teaspoon thyme
¼	teaspoon marjoram
1	minced celery stalk
8-10	peppercorns
	Grated lemon rind
½	cup sour cream (optional)

1. Combine red wine, vinegar, bay leaf, and sliced onion. Pour over pieces of rabbit in glass baking dish and marinate in refrigerator for at least 24 hours.
2. Remove and dry rabbit pieces and coat lightly with mixture of flour and salt. Reserve marinade. Melt butter in skillet and brown rabbit.
3. Place rabbit in slow cooker. Add marinade and remaining ingredients.

4. Cover and cook on Low 8-10 hours.
5. Thicken sauce with ½ cup sour cream or mixture of 1 tablespoon butter and 1 tablespoon flour. Serve with spaetzle or noodles.

Menu

Hasenpfeffer
Spaetzle
Green Beans and Almonds
German Chocolate Cake

Swiss Fondue

Cooking time: 1 hour

- 1 whole garlic clove
- 2¼ cups dry white wine (Rhine, Reisling, or Chablis)
- 1 pound grated Swiss cheese
- 1½ tablespoons flour
- ½ teaspoon salt
- Dash of white pepper
- ⅛ teaspoon nutmeg
- 3 tablespoons kirsch
- Loaf of French bread cut into 1-inch cubes
- Slice of cooked ham cut into cubes

1. Rub garlic clove over inside surface of slow cooker and discard. Pour in wine, cover, and heat on High 1 hour.
2. Mix flour with grated cheese and add to slow cooker when wine is heated. Stir well until cheese is melted. Stir in salt, pepper, nutmeg, and kirsch. Cook five minutes longer, turn to Low, and serve from table. Guests can spear French bread cubes and ham cubes and dip into cheese fondue.

Menu

Swiss Fondue
Salad of Mixed Greens
Chilled White Wine
Lime Sherbet

Ratatouille

Cooking time: 7-9 hours

- 2 large yellow onions, sliced
- 1 large eggplant, sliced
- 4 small zucchini, sliced
- 2 garlic cloves, minced
- 2 green peppers, seeded and cut in thin strips
- 6-8 large, ripe tomatoes, cut in half-inch wedges
- 1 teaspoon basil
- 2 teaspoons salt
- ¼ teaspoon freshly ground pepper
- 2 tablespoons chopped parsley
- ¼ cup olive oil

1. Layer half the vegetables in slow cooker in the following order: onion, eggplant, zucchini, garlic, green peppers, tomatoes. Repeat layers with remaining vegetables. Sprinkle basil, salt, pepper, and parsley on top. Drizzle olive oil over top.
2. Cover and cook on Low 7-9 hours. Cool and chop coarsely.

Menu

Ratatouille
Slices of Cold Ham
Potato Bread
Peppermint Ice Cream

7

Vegetables and Rice

The slow cooker is well suited to preparing a wide variety of vegetable dishes—from corn on the cob to mixed vegetable casseroles to dried peas.

Most fresh or frozen vegetables (including broccoli, asparagus, and cauliflower) can be prepared in the slow cooker with water, butter, and seasoning. Or vegetables may be wrapped in aluminum foil, which eliminates the need for stirring. Cook on High for a little under an hour and then turn to Low for 2-4 hours. Check the recipe book that accompanies your slow cooker for exact directions. Some slow-cooker manufacturers now also offer a special cooking accessory to be used in steaming vegetables.

By far the most famous regional dried bean dish is Boston baked beans, but almost every area of the United States has its specialty: Cuban black beans in the South, Louisiana red bean casserole, and in the Midwest a multitude of mixed bean casseroles. These delicious concoctions, perfect for picnics, buffets, and potluck dinners, have been ignored in recent years because few cooks have the leisure time to tend a pot for 12 to 24 hours. Happily, the slow cooker may rescue these traditional dishes from oblivion.

There are several ways to presoak dried beans before cooking. Soak them overnight, or, if it is more convenient, boil the beans for half an hour, then cover and let stand for an hour and a half. If your tap water is hard, add just a pinch of baking soda to the water before boiling to help soften beans.

Several vegetable and rice casseroles are also included here. These more elaborate dishes can help vary menu routine, but they can be prepared with a minimum of effort. You can leave a vegetable casserole in the slow cooker while you are working or shopping and serve it with broiled steak, fish fillet, or another simply prepared main dish.

Country Green Beans

Cooking time: 10-24 hours

- 2 pounds fresh green beans
- ⅛ cup bacon drippings
- 3 cups water
- 2 fresh ham hocks
- 1 teaspoon salt
- ¼ teaspoon basil
- 4 small white onions

1. Heat bacon drippings in skillet. Add beans and stir to coat. Transfer to slow cooker. Add water, ham hocks, salt, basil, and onions.
2. Cover and cook on Low 10-24 hours.

Americana Bean Bake

Cooking time: 6-8 hours

- ½ pound lima beans
- ½ pound dried navy or Great Northern beans
- 7 cups water
- 2 teaspoons salt
- ¼ pound bacon
- 1 large chopped onion
- ½ cup light molasses
- ½ cup chili sauce
- ¼ cup prepared mustard
- 1 8-ounce can tomato sauce

1. Rinse beans, picking out any discolored ones. Combine beans, salt and water in a large kettle; cover, bring to a boil, and boil 30 minutes. Remove from heat and let stand for 1½ hours.
2. Fry bacon. Drain on paper towel until cool. Crumble in small pieces. Pour off all but ¼ of bacon grease. Add onion and sauté lightly. Stir in molasses, chili sauce, and mustard. Bring to a boil and then remove from heat.
3. Drain beans. In slow cooker combine beans, bacon, and onion mixture and pour in tomato sauce. Stir well. Cover and cook on High 4-6 hours.

Black Bean Casserole

Cooking time: 9-15 hours

1 pound presoaked black beans
6 cups water
1 chopped garlic clove
½ cup chopped onion
1 teaspoon whole cumin seeds
1 pound ham hocks
½ teaspoon salt
¼ teaspoon pepper
Dash of cayenne

1. Place presoaked beans in slow cooker. Cover with water and add remaining ingredients.
2. Cover and cook on High for 3 hours; turn to Low and cook another 6-12 hours (or an additional 3-6 hours on High).

Boston Baked Beans

Cooking time: 12-14 hours

- 1 pound dried navy beans
- 6 cups cold water
- ¼ pound salt pork
- 1 medium onion stuck with 2 cloves
- 2 teaspoons dry mustard
- ½ cup brown sugar
- ¼ cup molasses
- 1 teaspoon salt
- ½ teaspoon pepper

1. Wash beans, place in large kettle, cover with 6 cups water, bring to a boil, and boil half an hour. Remove from heat. Cover and let stand 1½ hours.
2. Cut a slice from salt pork and place it in the bottom of the slow cooker. Drain beans, reserving liquid. Add beans to slow cooker placing onion stuck with 2 cloves in the center.
3. Mix mustard, brown sugar, molasses, and salt and pepper with 1 cup of bean liquid and pour over beans. Cut three gashes in remaining salt pork and place pork on top of beans, rind side on top.
4. Cover slow cooker and cook on Low 10-12 hours (High: 5-6 hours). Remove cover last half hour.

Lima Bean Bake

Cooking time: 8-11 hours

- 1 pound dried baby lima beans
- ½ cup chili sauce
- 3 tablespoons maple syrup

1 tablespoon curry powder
½ cup brown sugar
2½ cups water

1. Soak lima beans in water overnight.
2. Drain beans, reserving 2½ cups liquid, or enough to almost cover beans and place in slow cooker. Add rest of ingredients and stir.
3. Cover and bake on High for 1 hour; then turn to Low and cook 7-10 hours. (Or cook on High an additional 4-5 hours.)

Louisiana Beans

Cooking time: 10-12 hours

1 pound presoaked dried red beans or kidney beans
4 cups water
2 teaspoons salt
Dash of cayenne pepper
1 medium onion stuck with two cloves
2 minced garlic cloves
2 chopped celery stalks
½ cup finely chopped parsley
2 crumbled bay leaves
2 teaspoons chili powder
2 teaspoons Worcestershire sauce
2 1-pound 13-ounce cans tomatoes with liquid
2 cups cooked long grain rice

1. In slow cooker, combine presoaked beans with remaining ingredients, except rice.
2. Cover and cook on High 2 hours; turn to Low and cook an additional 8-10 hours. Add cooked rice during last hour.

Braised Red Cabbage

Cooking time: 8-10 hours

1 medium head of red cabbage (about 2½-3 pounds)
4 tablespoons butter
1 tablespoon sugar
1 teaspoon salt
¼ teaspoon pepper
⅓ cup water
⅓ cup red wine vinegar
2 sliced apples

1. Wash cabbage head in cold water, remove outer leaves, core, and slice.
2. Combine butter, sugar, salt, pepper, water, and vinegar in a saucepan. Bring to a boil and cook until the butter has melted completely. Place alternate layers of sliced apples and cabbage in slow cooker. Pour vinegar mixture over cabbage.
3. Cover and cook on Low 8-10 hours. Serves 6.

Under-cover Carrots

Cooking time: 3-5 hours

12 medium sliced carrots
1 small sliced onion
¼ cup butter
¼ cup all-purpose flour
1 teaspoon salt
½ teaspoon dry mustard

2 cups milk
Freshly ground pepper
¼ teaspoon celery salt
½ pound coarsely grated Cheddar cheese
3 cups buttered fresh bread crumbs

1. In skillet, melt butter and sauté onion until golden. Stir in flour, salt, and dry mustard. Gradually stir in milk and cook over low heat until smooth. Add pepper and celery salt.
2. In slow cooker, arrange a layer of carrots followed by a layer of cheese. Cover with mustard sauce from the skillet. Top with buttered bread crumbs.
3. Cover and cook on High for 1 hour. Turn to Low and cook an additional 2-4 hours. Serves 6-8.

Corn on the Cob

Cooking time: 2½-3 hours

6-8 ears of fresh corn on the cob
1 tablespoon sugar
½ cup water

1. Remove corn silk but leave green outer husks on each ear of corn. Wash husks and cut ears to fit in slow cooker. Add sugar and water.
2. Cover and cook on High 1 hour; turn to Low and cook an additional 1½-2 hours. To serve, remove husks.

Eggplant Casserole

Cooking time: 6-8 hours

1 large eggplant cut in half-inch slices
4 tablespoons olive oil
Salt
Freshly ground pepper
1 teaspoon dried basil
1 large thinly sliced onion
1 garlic clove, slivered
2 8-ounce cans tomato sauce
1 finely chopped green pepper
½ cup toasted bread crumbs
1 cup grated Parmesan cheese

1. Heat oil in skillet and quickly brown eggplant slices a few at a time. Add more olive oil if necessary. Salt and pepper to taste and sprinkle with basil. Sauté onion and garlic in olive oil until just limp.
2. Arrange layers of tomato sauce, eggplant, onion-garlic mixture, and chopped green pepper in slow cooker. Sprinkle a little cheese over each layer. Scatter toasted bread crumbs over top.
3. Cover and cook on Low 6-8 hours.

Baked Onions

Cooking time: 3-5 hours

24 small white boiling onions
3 tablespoons butter
3 tablespoons brown sugar

1 teaspoon salt
¼ teaspoon nutmeg
4 whole cloves
Dash of cayenne
Dash of white pepper
¼ cup toasted, slivered blanched almonds

1. Peel onions and cook in boiling, salted water for five minutes. Drain.
2. Melt butter in preheated slow cooker. Stir in brown sugar, salt, nutmeg, cloves, cayenne, and white pepper. Add onions and stir to coat with mixture.
3. Cover slow cooker and cook on High 1 hour, turn to Low and cook another 2-4 hours.
4. Before serving, remove cloves, spoon sauce over onions, and sprinkle with almonds.

Corn-stuffed Peppers

Cooking time: 6-8 hours

6 green peppers
2 cups canned or frozen corn, drained
1 cup dry bread crumbs
1 small minced onion
1 small jar pimientos
1 6-ounce can tomato sauce
½ teaspoon salt
¼ teaspoon pepper
¼ cup tomato paste
½ cup water

1. Cut top off green peppers and remove seeds and membranes. Combine corn, bread crumbs, onion, pimientos, tomato sauce, salt, and pepper. Stuff peppers with corn mixture and place in bottom of slow cooker. Pour in tomato paste and water.
2. Cover and cook on Low 6-8 hours (High: 3 hours).

Baked Potatoes

Cooking time: 8-10 hours

Scrub and butter baking potatoes (as many as you need or as will fit in the slow cooker.) Cover and cook on Low without water for 8-10 hours.

Apple-Sweet Potato Casserole

Cooking time: 4-6 hours

2 cups boiled sliced sweet potatoes
2 medium apples sliced one-quarter-inch thick
¾ cup brown sugar
½ cup water
4 tablespoons butter or margarine
3 tablespoons lemon juice

1. Boil ¼ cup of brown sugar and water in saucepan 3 minutes or until sugar is dissolved.
2. Place apples in brown sugar syrup a few at a time. Cover pan and simmer until apples are soft. Remove apples and save syrup.

3. Sprinkle a little brown sugar into slow cooker. Arrange alternate layers of potatoes and apples, ending with potatoes. Dot apple layers with butter and sprinkle with brown sugar. Dot top layer with butter and sugar. Stir lemon juice into brown sugar syrup and pour over casserole.
4. Cover and cook on Low 4-6 hours.

Spinach Loaf

Cooking time: 5-6 hours

- 2 pounds fresh spinach
- 1 small chopped onion
- 3 tablespoons butter or margarine
- ¼ cup flour
- ¾ cup milk
- ¾ cup bread crumbs
- 2 eggs, separated
- 1 teaspoon salt
- 1 teaspoon sugar
- ¼ teaspoon dried rosemary
- ½ teaspoon black pepper

1. Wash spinach and cook in water in saucepan until tender. Drain, chop fine, and return to pan.
2. In skillet, sauté onion in butter or margarine; blend in flour. Gradually add milk. Cook until thick, stirring constantly. Pour sauce over spinach, add crumbs and stir well.
3. Beat egg yolks until creamy. Add yolks, salt, sugar, rosemary, and pepper to spinach. Beat egg whites until stiff. Fold in beaten egg whites. Transfer spinach mixture to buttered slow cooker.
4. Cover and cook on High 1 hour; turn to Low and cook an additional 4-5 hours.

Squash Boats

Cooking time: 7-9 hours

- 2-3 acorn squash
- 2 tablespoons butter, melted
- Salt and pepper
- 1 1-pound 2-ounce can sliced apples for pie
- ¾ cup brown sugar
- 1 teaspoon lemon juice
- ¼ teaspoon ground ginger
- ¼ teaspoon ground cinnamon
- 2-3 tablespoons butter or margarine
- ¼ cup water

1. Cut squash in half and remove seeds. Brush insides with melted butter and season with salt and pepper.
2. Combine apple slices, brown sugar, lemon juice, ginger, and cinnamon. Spoon this mixture into each squash half. Dot with butter. Pour ¼ cup water into slow cooker. Wrap each squash half in aluminum foil and place in bottom of slow cooker.
3. Cover and cook on High 1 hour; turn to Low and cook another 6-8 hours until squash is tender.

Glazed Turnips

Cooking time: 8-10 hours

- 2 medium peeled and sliced yellow turnips
- 1 cup boiling salted water
- 1 cup brown sugar

½ cup orange juice
1 teaspoon grated orange rind
2 tablespoons butter

Place all ingredients in slow cooker, stir well, cover, and cook on Low 8-10 hours.

Green Rice Casserole

Cooking time: 5-7 hours

1½ cups evaporated milk
½ cup melted butter or margarine
3 eggs
3 cups cooked long grain rice
1 cup chopped parsley
1½ cups finely chopped spinach leaves
½ cup minced scallions
Salt and white pepper to taste
1 cup grated Parmesan cheese

1. Combine evaporated milk, melted butter, and eggs. Beat until frothy and well mixed. Add remaining ingredients and stir thoroughly.
2. Grease slow cooker. Transfer ingredients to slow cooker, cover, and cook on High 1 hour; turn to Low and cook an additional 4-6 hours. Stir several times during first hour.

Rice Jambalaya

Cooking time: 4-6 hours

2 slices bacon
1 pound sliced mushrooms
2 medium chopped green peppers

1 medium chopped onion
1 chopped celery stalk
1 tablespoon flour
Water
1½ cups raw long grain rice
2 small jars pimientos
2 cups canned tomatoes with juice
1 teaspoon salt
Dash of cayenne
½ teaspoon paprika

1. In skillet over medium heat, sauté bacon lightly. Add mushrooms, green peppers, onion, and celery and cook until soft. Stir in flour and cook until brown. Transfer skillet mixture to slow cooker.
2. Add enough water to juice from tomato cans to make 1½ cups liquid and add to slow cooker along with remaining ingredients. Stir well.
3. Cover and cook on Low 4-6 hours (High 2-3 hours).

8

Fruits, Desserts, and Confections

With the aid of the slow cooker, you can prepare elegant and unusual fruit dishes and desserts with little effort. Once again, the slow cooker saves time where it counts, right before mealtime. Start fruit dishes and desserts in the morning or at noon so they are warm and ready for serving when you're ready for dessert. Because the timing is not crucial, you can hold the dessert to serve later if everyone is too full immediately after dinner.

Most of the recipes selected are for foods that you can't buy already prepared and are designed to be cooked with a minimum of effort. A couple of easy candy recipes are also included.

Baked Apples in Wine

Cooking time: 8 hours

6 apples
6 tablespoons currant jelly
1 cup dry white wine
¼ cup sugar
2 tablespoons butter

1. Peel apples and core to within about an inch of the bottom. Place one tablespoon of currant jelly in each core. Transfer to slow cooker. Combine wine and sugar and pour over the apples. Dot with butter.
2. Cover slow cooker and cook on Low 8 hours.

Dutch Apple Bake

Cooking time: 8-10 hours

½ pound peeled and sliced cooking apples
¼ cup sugar
1½ tablespoons lemon juice
½ cup honey
½ cup flour
¼ cup brown sugar
¼ teaspoon salt
½ teaspoon cinnamon
Pinch of ground cloves
¼ cup butter or margarine

1. Arrange sliced apples in bottom of slow cooker. Sprinkle sugar and lemon juice on top. Pour honey over all.

2. Combine flour, brown sugar, salt, cinnamon, and cloves and stir well. Cut in butter until mixture is consistency of coarse cornmeal. Sprinkle brown sugar mixture over apples.
3. Cover and cook on Low 8-10 hours or until top crust is browned. Serve warm with ice cream or top with whipped cream.

Chunky Applesauce

Cooking time: 8-10 hours

8-10	large cooking apples
½	cup water
½-1	cup sugar
2	slices lemon
1	teaspoon cinnamon

1. Peel, core, and cut apples into small chunks. Place in slow cooker with water, ½ cup sugar, and lemon slices.
2. Cover and cook on Low 8-10 hours. When applesauce is cooked, remove lemon slices. Stir in cinnamon and more sugar if desired.

Baked Peaches in Bourbon

Cooking time: 4-6 hours

4	fresh peaches
2	cups brown sugar
1	cup water
4	cloves
½	cup bourbon
½	pint whipping cream

1. Place water and brown sugar in slow cooker. Cover and cook on High until sugar dissolves.
2. Pour boiling water over peaches and peel. Halve peaches, remove pits, insert a clove in the top of each peach. Place in slow cooker.
3. Cover and cook on Low 4-6 hours, turning peaches occasionally.
4. Approximately half an hour before serving, stir in bourbon. Remove cloves and place peach in dessert dish. Pour liquid from pot over top. Serve with whipped cream.

Baked Pears

Cooking time: 4-6 hours

- 3 peeled, cored, and halved pears
- 1 cup water
- 1½ cups light brown sugar firmly packed
- ¼ cup raisins
- 2 tablespoons finely chopped walnuts
- 2 tablespoons granulated sugar
- 1 tablespoon lemon juice
- 2 teaspoons cinnamon
- Pear brandy (optional)

1. Put water and brown sugar into slow cooker, cover, and cook on High until sugar is dissolved.
2. Mix together raisins, walnuts, granulated sugar, and lemon juice. Place spoonful of this mixture into hollow of each pear half. Place pears in slow cooker. Sprinkle cinnamon over tops of pears.
3. Cover and cook on Low 4-6 hours, basting several times.
4. When pears are tender, remove and serve. If desired, pour a little pear brandy over the pears just before serving.

Pears in Port Wine

Cooking time: 4-6 hours

6 peeled pears with stems intact
2 cups port or sherry wine
½ cup sugar
3 slices lemon
3 slices orange

1. Pour wine into slow cooker; add sugar, cover, and cook on High until sugar is dissolved. Place pears in liquid, turning to coat well. Add lemon and orange slices.
2. Cover and cook on Low 4-6 hours. Turn occasionally.
3. When pears are tender, serve with wine sauce poured over them. They may be served warm, but they are best when chilled in wine sauce first.

Dried Prunes

Cooking time: 8-9 hours

½ pound dried prunes
Water to cover
3 tablespoons brown sugar
¼ teaspoon cinnamon
3 slices lemon
½ pint commercial sour cream

1. Place prunes in slow cooker. Add water to cover (or amount specified on package). Sprinkle with sugar and cinnamon; arrange lemon slices on top.

2. Cover and cook on Low 8-9 hours. Remove lemon slices and serve warm with sour cream.

Baked Rhubarb Dessert

Cooking time: 4-6 hours

- 1½ pounds rhubarb
- ½ cup sugar
- ½ teaspoon powdered ginger
- ½ cup strawberry jam
- ¼ cup water
- 1 cup fresh strawberries
- Heavy cream

1. Remove leaves from rhubarb, wash, and cut into 2-inch slices. Place half of rhubarb in bottom of slow cooker. Sprinkle with ¼ cup sugar and ¼ teaspoon ginger. Spoon on ¼ cup of jam. Add a second layer of rhubarb and top with remaining sugar, ginger, and jam.
2. Cover and cook on Low 4-6 hours. Serve with fresh strawberries and cream.

Curried Fruit

Cooking time: 7-8 hours

- 2 pounds dried apricot halves
- 1 cup sultana raisins
- 1 13½-ounce can pineapple chunks, undrained
- ⅓ cup butter, melted
- ¼ teaspoon ground cloves

- ¼ teaspoon cinnamon
- 1 tablespoon curry powder
- ¼ cup white wine
- 2 cups water
- 1 cup freshly grated coconut

1. Place all ingredients except coconut in slow cooker. Stir thoroughly, cover, and cook on Low 7-8 hours.
2. Garnish with coconut and serve warm with main course or as dessert with a scoop of vanilla ice cream.

Mixed Fruit Casserole

Cooking Time: 7-8 hours

- 1 cup graham cracker crumbs
- ½ cup chopped pecans
- ½ cup brown sugar firmly packed
- 1 tablespoon orange juice
- 1 teaspoon grated orange rind
- 2 peeled, cored, and sliced apples
- 2 peeled and sliced peaches

Hard Sauce

- ¼ cup butter
- ¾ cup brown sugar
- 1-2 tablespoons brandy

1. Toss ingredients lightly together and place in slow cooker. Cover and cook on Low 7-8 hours.
2. Cream butter and brown sugar together. Add brandy to taste. Chill hard sauce.
3. Serve fruit warm with chilled hard sauce.

Chocolate Pudding

Cooking time: 3½-4½ hours

- 1 tablespoon butter
- 2 ounces semi-sweet chocolate
- 1 cup sifted sugar
- 1 beaten egg
- 1 cup coffee
- 1 tablespoon rum
- 1½ cups sifted all-purpose flour
- ½ teaspoon salt
- 1½ teaspoons baking powder
- ⅔ cup ground, blanched almonds
- ½ cup light raisins
- ½ teaspoon vanilla
- ½ pint whipping cream

1. Melt chocolate and butter in small saucepan over very low heat.
2. Add sugar slowly to beaten egg. Add melted butter and chocolate, coffee, and rum.
3. Sift flour with salt and baking powder. Stir into chocolate mixture. Fold in nuts and raisins. Add vanilla.
4. Grease a 2-pound coffee can. Pour in pudding mixture until ⅔ full. Place can in slow cooker and cover top of can with 4-6 paper towels.
5. Cover and cook on High 3½-4½ hours.
6. Remove pudding from slow cooker. Let stand 10 minutes and then turn out on serving platter. Serve immediately with whipped cream. Serves 6.

Holiday Pudding

Cooking time: 4-5 hours

- ½ pound ground beef suet
- 2 cups fine dry bread crumbs

1 cup sifted all-purpose flour
1 cup sugar
1 cup finely chopped, blanched almonds
1 cup currants
½ cup light raisins
½ cup dark raisins
⅔ cup mixed candied fruits
1 teaspoon each ground nutmeg, cinnamon, and salt
¼ teaspoon ground allspice
¾ cup milk
4 slightly beaten eggs
½ cup brandy or rum
1½ teaspoons grated lemon peel
¼ cup lemon juice

1. Mix together suet, crumbs, flour, sugar, almonds, currants, raisins, candied fruit, spices, and salt.
2. In a separate bowl, combine milk, slightly beaten eggs, brandy or rum, lemon peel, and lemon juice. Stir well and combine with fruit mixture.
3. Grease 2-quart mold or 2-pound coffee can. Dust lightly with flour. Pour mixture into mold and place mold in slow cooker. Cover top of mold with 4-6 paper towels.
4. Cover slow cooker and cook on High 4-5 hours until suet is absorbed. Do not uncover slow cooker until last hour. Serve with hard sauce. (See index.)

Chocolate Caramel Candy

Cooking time: 12-13 hours

3 cups sugar
1 cup light corn syrup
1 14-ounce can evaporated milk
3 ounces semi-sweet chocolate

- ½ cup butter
- 2 teaspoons vanilla
- 1 cup chopped almonds

1. Mix together sugar, corn syrup, evaporated milk, chocolate, and butter.
2. Cover and cook on High 4-5 hours, stirring several times. Turn to Low, remove cover and cook overnight (or until the caramel coats a spoon). Add vanilla and almonds.
3. Pour caramel onto buttered cookie sheet. (The cookie sheet should have four sides and be at least ½″ deep.) Cool until set. Cut into squares.

Peppermint Wafers

Cooking time: 1 hour

- 1 pound of confectioners' 10-X powdered sugar
- 3 tablespoons light corn syrup
- ½ teaspoon peppermint extract
- 3 tablespoons water
- 1 drop of red or green food coloring

1. In slow cooker, mix together confectioners' sugar and corn syrup. Cover and cook on Low 1 hour or until of smooth consistency. Add peppermint extract and stir. Leave slow cooker on Low while you make wafers.
2. Using a soup spoon, drop mixture onto cookie sheet lined with waxed paper. Wafer should be approximately 1-inch round.
3. When half the mixture has been used, color the remaining candy green or pink and make remaining wafers as in step 2. Allow candy to set at room temperature.

4. When almost firm, press fork into top to make ridges. For Christmas decoration, mix a little confectioners' sugar and water in small bowls to make frosting. Color frosting red, green, and yellow. With toothpick, drop frosting on wafers to make designs—flowers, Christmas trees or bells. Makes 2 dozen candies.

9

Fondue

The slow cooker's low heat settings can heat and keep warm cheese fondue, dessert fondue, and hot dips for crackers and snacks, and it's safer than a fondue pot heated by an open flame. Small slow cookers (approximately 2 quarts) and casserole-style cooker are convenient for family dinners or small dinner parties. Larger models hold party-sized quantities.

In addition to the traditional meat or cheese fondue, there are a variety of appetizer and dessert fondue dishes. These are fun not only for family meals but are ideal for parties. You might serve strawberry or blueberry fondue as a buffet brunch for house guests or family. Set out a bowl of waffle squares (preferably on a warming tray), bananas, pineapples and strawberries, plus a big platter of sausages and a pot of steaming black coffee.

The beauty of fondue is that it can be prepared ahead of time with little effort, then set out to enjoy. It will stay warm and delicious for hours.

Two-Cheese Fondue

Cooking time: 1-6 hours

- 2 8-ounce packages sharp natural Cheddar cheese, grated
- 1 8-ounce package natural Swiss cheese, grated
- 1 small garlic clove, halved
- 1 tablespoon all-purpose flour
- ¾ cup of beer
- ½ teaspoon dry mustard
- Dash of Mexican hot pepper sauce

1. Rub inside of slow cooker with garlic; discard garlic. Toss flour with grated cheese. Heat beer in slow cooker; slowly add cheese, stirring constantly. Stir in hot pepper sauce and dry mustard.
2. Cover and cook on Low 1-6 hours. If fondue becomes thick, slowly stir in a little more beer.

Fondue Rarebit

Cooking time: 2-3 hours

- 2 8-ounce packages processed caraway cheese, coarsely grated
- 3 tablespoons cornstarch
- ¼ teaspoon dry mustard
- 1 12-ounce can of beer
- 1 tablespoon caraway seeds
- 1 teaspoon Worcestershire sauce
- Dash of cayenne pepper
- ½ garlic clove, crushed

3 cups French bread cubes
1 12-ounce package frozen shrimp, thawed and cooked
Cauliflower buds

1. Stir together cornstarch and dry mustard in slow cooker. Gradually stir in ¼ cup beer to make a smooth paste. Slowly add rest of beer. Add caraway seeds, Worcestershire, cayenne, garlic, and grated cheese.
2. Cover slow cooker and cook on Low 2-3 hours.
3. Cook cauliflower buds in rapidly boiling water for 7 minutes *only.* Spear shrimp, bread cubes, and cauliflower buds on fondue forks and dip into fondue. This may also be served as a main dish over toast.

Mocha Fondue

Cooking time: 1-6 hours

18 ounces milk chocolate
1 cup whipping cream
4 tablespoons rum or kirsch
Pinch of cinnamon
1 tablespoon instant coffee

1. Place all ingredients in slow cooker, stir well, cover, and set to High.
2. Cook on High for 45 minutes. Stir again and serve. Cooker can be left on Low to keep warm for 6 hours. If you like chocolate less sweet, substitute semisweet chocolate.

(Leftover fondue can be stored in a glass jar in the refrigerator and reheated for ice cream topping.)

Blueberry Fondue

Cooking time: 1-5 hours

- 2 cups frozen blueberries
- ¼ cup each sugar and water
- 2 tablespoons lime juice
- 2 teaspoons cornstarch
- ½ teaspoon cinnamon

1. Place all ingredients in slow cooker, cover, and cook on High 1 hour or until mixture is thickened.
2. Turn to Low for serving. This may be used as a dip for banana slices, pineapple chunks, toasted waffle squares, and/or strawberries.

Candy Apple Fondue

Cooking time: 1 hour

- 2 8-ounce jars butterscotch ice cream topping
- 6 apples
- 1½ cups finely chopped walnuts or pecans

1. Heat butterscotch topping in slow cooker set on High for one hour.
2. Core, quarter, and cube apples. Spear cubes on fondue forks, dip into butterscotch and then into chopped nuts.

Orange Fondue

Cooking time: 1-6 hours

- 1 cup orange juice
- 1 cup sugar

3 tablespoons cornstarch
Dash of salt
¼ cup unsweetened pineapple juice
3 tablespoons lemon juice
¼ cup hot water
1 tablespoon butter or margarine
1 teaspoon grated lemon peel

1. In saucepan, combine sugar, cornstarch, and salt. Gradually add orange juice, pineapple juice, lemon juice, and water. Heat to boiling and boil one minute stirring constantly. Remove saucepan from heat. Stir in butter or margarine and grated lemon peel. Pour into slow cooker.
2. Cover and cook for 1-6 hours.
3. Into this mixture you may dip apple cubes, gingerbread cubes, cream cheese cubes, banana slices, cantaloupe balls, and/or doughnut holes.

Strawberry Fondue

Cooking time: 1-5 hours

2 10-ounce packages frozen strawberries, thawed
1 cup currant jelly
2 tablespoons cornstarch
1 tablespoon water
2 tablespoons brandy or Cointreau

1. Combine thawed strawberries, currant jelly, cornstarch, and water in small saucepan. Bring to a boil and boil one minute, stirring constantly. Transfer fondue to slow cooker. Stir in brandy or Cointreau.
2. Cover and cook on Low 1-5 hours. Makes approximately 2½ cups.

Hot Bean Dip

Cooking time: 1 hour

- 2 10-ounce cans condensed black bean soup
- 2 8-ounce cans tomato sauce
- 1 cup shredded Cheddar cheese
- ½ teaspoon chili powder
- 2 teaspoons Worcestershire sauce

Place ingredients in slow cooker, stir well, cover, and cook on Low 1 hour. Stir again, serve, leaving cooker set on Low from 2-6 hours. Use as dip for corn chips or tortilla chips.

10

Potpourri

Included in this final chapter are a mix of recipes that will show you many ways to take advantage of the slow cooker's basic principle: slow, moist cooking. From the few examples given here, you can easily adapt a wide variety of similar recipes. For instance, the method for cooking strawberry preserves can be used for many other fruits, and there are a great many more easy, no-knead breads in addition to the ones included here.

Hot cereals can be prepared conveniently in the slow cooker. Mix them up the night before and cook overnight. Everybody in the family can have a hot breakfast whenever he or she is hungry, whether the cook is awake yet or not.

Convenience is also the key word in preparing sauces, fruit butters, chutneys, and hot drinks the slow cooker way. The imcomparable flavor of grandmother's homemade "recipes" can now be enjoyed without the hard work and constant attention they required from her.

Apple Butter

Cooking time: 16-20 hours

- 6 pounds apples
- Water
- Sugar
- 2 teaspoons ground cinnamon
- ½ teaspoon ground cloves
- Juice of one lemon

1. Peel, core, and quarter apples and place in slow cooker. Nearly cover with water. Cover and cook on Low 8-10 hours until soft.
2. Purée apples in blender. To each cup of pulp add ½ cup sugar. Add remaining ingredients. Return to slow cooker. Cover and cook on Low 8-10 hours. Remove cover during last half hour. If thick butter is desired, leave cover off slow cooker the entire time.

Peach Butter

Cooking time: 16-20 hours

- 4 pounds peaches
- ½ cup water
- Sugar
- 2 teaspoons ginger
- ½ teaspoon ground cloves
- Juice of one lemon

1. Peel, quarter, and remove pits from peaches. Place in slow cooker with ½ cup water and cook on Low 8-10 hours.

2. Purée peaches in blender. Add ½ cup sugar for each cup of pulp. Add remaining ingredients and cook as for apple butter.

(To simplify, substitute canned water-packed peaches that have been drained and go right to step 2.)

Apples and Oatmeal

Cooking time: 8-9 hours

- 1 apple, peeled, cored, and sliced
- ¼ cup brown sugar
- 2 teaspoons cinnamon
- 2 cups old-fashioned uncooked oatmeal
- 4 cups water
- 1 tablespoon salt

1. Roll apple slices in mixture of brown sugar and cinnamon to coat. Mix oatmeal with water and salt (or according to package directions). Arrange apples in layer on bottom of slow cooker. Add oatmeal mixture.
2. Cover and cook overnight (8-9 hours) on Low. Just before serving, stir apples and oatmeal thoroughly. Serve with milk and additional brown sugar. Makes 6 cups.

(Other cereals which may be cooked in slow cooker overnight include cornmeal mush, grits, and cracked wheat.)

Chili Sauce

Cooking time: 12-18 hours

- 24 large ripe tomatoes
- 4 large onions

4 green peppers, cored, seeded, and chopped
1 tablespoon ground cloves
1 teaspoon ground allspice
Pinch of cayenne
5 cups cider vinegar
8 tablespoons sugar
2 tablespoons salt
1 tablespoon cinnamon

(This excellent sauce may be served with pot roast, meat loaf, cold ham, or pork loin.)

1. Purée tomatoes a few at a time in blender. Place in slow cooker. Purée onions and peppers in blender. Add to cooker. Add remaining ingredients and stir.
2. Cover and cook on Low 12-18 hours (5-6 hours on High). Remove the cover the last hour to thicken sauce.
3. Put into sterilized jars and seal. Boil on rack in large canning kettle for 30 minutes. Store in a cool, dry place. Makes approximately 2½ quarts.

Sweet and Sour Cocktail Meatballs

Cooking time: 1 hour

1 pound ground beef
1 can finely chopped water chestnuts
Minced onions
Salt and pepper
Oregano
2 teaspoons olive oil
1 8-12-ounce jar chili sauce
1 10-ounce jar grape jelly

1. Mix beef, water chestnuts, onions, salt, pepper, and oregano and make into small meatballs. Fry meatballs in small amount of olive oil; pour off pan drippings.
2. Put chili sauce and jelly into large saucepan; heat until jelly liquefies. Transfer to slow cooker and add meatballs to sauce.
3. Cover and cook on High 1 hour. Serve immediately or refrigerate or freeze in baking dish until ready to serve; then reheat in slow cooker.

Peach Chutney

Cooking time: 8-10 hours

5-6 fresh peaches, peeled, pitted, and sliced
1 large chopped onion
½ cup seedless raisins
1 cup brown sugar firmly packed
1½ cups white vinegar
¼ cup chopped preserved ginger
¼ cup chopped candied lemon peel
½ teaspoon salt
¼ teaspoon powdered cloves
¼ teaspoon grated nutmeg
¼-½ teaspoon cayenne
¼ teaspoon black pepper

(Serve this as a condiment with barbecued meats and curry dishes.)

1. Add all ingredients to slow cooker. Cover and cook on Low 8-10 hours. Remove cover during last hour of cooking.
2. Seal in hot sterile jars. Makes 2 pints.

Strawberry Preserves

Cooking time: 8-10 hours

4 cups whole strawberries, hulled
4 cups sugar
1 lemon

1. Sqeeze lemon (reserving juice) and grate lemon rind. In slow cooker, arrange layers of fruit and sugar as follows: 2 cups strawberries, 2 cups sugar, half of lemon juice and rind, 2 cups strawberries, 2 cups sugar and the rest of the lemon juice and rind.
2. Cover and cook on Low 8-10 hours. If thick preserves are desired, remove cover during last hour. Store in sterile pint canning jars or jelly jars sealed with paraffin.

(To make *peach preserves,* follow recipe for strawberry preserves, except use 4 cups of sliced peaches to 3 cups sugar.)

Corn Bread Stuffing

Cooking time: 5-9 hours

7 cups crumbled corn bread
1 cup stale wheat bread crumbs
10 tablespoons butter
3 chopped stalks celery
1 large chopped onion
1 teaspoon salt
½ teaspoon pepper
Pinch of poultry seasoning
2 slightly beaten eggs

Chicken broth
2 strips bacon, cooked and crumbled

1. Melt butter in skillet and sauté celery and onion until golden. Combine corn bread crumbs and wheat bread crumbs in large bowl. Pour butter mixture over crumbs. Season with salt, pepper, and poultry seasoning. Add eggs and mix well. Add just enough chicken broth to moisten slightly. Stir in bacon bits. Pack stuffing into slow cooker.
2. Cover and cook on High 45 minutes; turn to Low and cook another 4-8 hours.

Boston Brown Bread

Cooking time: 4-5 hours

½ cup rye flour
½ cup cornmeal
½ cup whole wheat flour
½ teaspoon salt
½ teaspoon baking soda
½ teaspoon baking powder
1 cup buttermilk
½ cup dark molasses
½ cup dark seedless raisins

1. Mix together rye flour, cornmeal, whole wheat flour, salt, baking soda, and baking powder. In another bowl, beat buttermilk and molasses until well blended. Gradually add dry ingredients. Stir in raisins.
2. Spoon mixture into greased two-pound coffee can. Place aluminum foil tightly over top of coffee can. Pour two cups of water into slow cooker. Set can in cooker.

3. Cover slow cooker and bake on High 4-5 hours. Remove can from cooker and let it cool one hour before unmolding.

Banana Bread

Cooking time: 3½-4½ hours

- 1 cup mashed ripe bananas (about 2)
- ½ cup butter
- 1 cup granulated sugar
- 2 well-beaten eggs
- 2 cups sifted all-purpose flour
- 2 teaspoons baking powder
- ½ teaspoon salt
- ⅓ cup milk
- 1 teaspoon lemon juice
- ½ cup chopped nuts

1. Cream butter and sugar. Stir in beaten eggs and banana pulp.
2. In large mixing bowl, sift flour with baking powder and salt.
3. In another bowl, combine milk and lemon juice, which will curdle.
4. Fold approximately ⅓ of the banana mixture into the dry ingredients, followed by ⅓ of the milk mixture. Alternate folding in these ingredients until all ingredients are mixed together. Stir in nuts. Pour into greased 2-pound coffee can.
5. Place can in slow cooker. Cover top of can with 4-6 paper towels.
6. Cover slow cooker and bake on High 3½-4½ hours. Do not lift cover until last hour.

Mrs. Grundy's Carrot Bread

Cooking time: 3½-4½ hours

- 1½ cups grated carrots
- 1 cup white sugar

- ¾ cup vegetable oil
- 2 well-beaten eggs
- 1½ cups flour
- 1 teaspoon baking soda
- ½ teaspoon nutmeg
- 1 teaspoon cinnamon
- ½ teaspoon salt
- ½ cup chopped nuts

1. Cream vegetable oil and sugar. Stir in eggs. Combine flour, soda, nutmeg, cinnamon, and salt. Sift into egg mixture. Fold in grated carrots and nuts. Spoon batter into 2-pound coffee can.
2. Follow cooking directions for banana bread (steps 5 and 6).

Cranberry Bread

Cooking time: 3½-4½ hours

- 1 cup halved cranberries
- 2 cups flour
- 1 cup sugar
- ½ teaspoon salt
- ½ teaspoon soda
- 1½ teaspoons baking powder
- 1 beaten egg
- 2 tablespoons butter, melted
- ½ cup orange juice
- 2 tablespoons hot water
- ½ cup chopped nuts
- 1 grated orange rind

1. In a large bowl, mix together flour, sugar, salt, soda, and baking powder. In another bowl, combine egg, butter, orange juice, and hot water. Add this to dry ingredients and

stir well. Stir in nuts, cranberries, and orange rind. Pour into greased 2-pound coffee can.

2. Follow cooking directions for banana bread (steps 5 and 6).

Pumpkin Bread

Cooking time: 3½-4½ hours

- 1 cup canned pumpkin
- ¼ cup shortening
- 1 cup sugar
- 1 well-beaten egg
- 2 cups flour
- 1 teaspoon ground cinnamon
- ½ teaspoon nutmeg
- ½ teaspoon ginger
- ¼ teaspoon salt
- ½ teaspoon baking powder
- 2 teaspoons baking soda
- ¼ cup chopped walnuts

1. Cream shortening and sugar. Add pumpkin and beaten egg. Combine dry ingredients except walnuts and sift into pumpkin mixture. Beat until smooth. Add walnuts. Spoon batter into greased 2-pound coffee can.
2. Follow cooking directions for banana bread (steps 5 and 6). Serve as bread with meal, or serve warm with whipped cream as a dessert.

Hot Buttered Rum

Cooking time: 5-10 hours

- 2 cups light brown sugar
- 1 finely grated lemon rind

1½ teaspoons cinnamon
½ teaspoon nutmeg
2-3 cups light rum
2 quarts hot water
Sweet butter
Cinnamon sticks, one for each serving

1. Place all ingredients except butter and cinnamon sticks in slow cooker. Stir well.
2. Cover and cook on High 2 hours; turn to Low and cook an additional 3-8 hours. Serve in mugs with a stick of cinnamon and 1 teaspoon warm butter. Makes about 12 cups.

Wassail Bowl

Cooking time: 5-9 hours

2 quarts cider
1 cup dark rum
¼ pound dark brown sugar
2 teaspoons whole allspice
1 teaspoon cloves
1 stick cinnamon
1 blade mace
½ teaspoon salt
1 thinly sliced lemon
1 large thinly sliced orange

1. Put cider, rum, and brown sugar in slow cooker. Tie allspice, cloves, cinnamon, and mace in cheesecloth bag. Add to cider. Add salt.
2. Cover and cook on High 1 hour; turn to Low and cook for an additional 4-8 hours. Remove spice bag. Add lemon and orange slices and serve warm. Makes about 12 cups.

Scramble Party Mix

Cooking time: 5-6 hours

2 cups Wheat Chex
2 cups Rice Chex
2 cups Corn Chex
2 cups mixed nuts
2 cups Cheerios
2 cups pretzel sticks
½ cup (1 stick) butter or margarine, melted
½-1 teaspoon salt
1 teaspoon garlic salt
5 teaspoons Worcestershire sauce

1. Place melted margarine, salt, garlic salt, and Worcestershire sauce in slow cooker and mix well. Add dry ingredients stirring thoroughly.
2. Cook uncovered on Low about 5 or 6 hours, stirring occasionally, until warm and crisp.

Index